Book of the American Colonies

BROWN PAPER SCHOOL

USKids History: Book of the American Colonies

Written by Howard Egger-Bovet *and* Marlene Smith-Baranzini

James J. Rawls, *Consulting Editor*

Illustrated by D. J. Simison

Little, Brown and Company

Boston   New York   Toronto   London

A Yolla Bolly Press Book

Brown Paper School USKids History: Book of the American Colonies was edited and prepared for publication at The Yolla Bolly Press, Covelo, California. This series is under the supervision of James Robertson and Carolyn Robertson. Production staff: Diana Fairbanks, Renée Menge, and Alexandra Chappell. Composition by Wilsted & Taylor, Oakland, California.

FIRST EDITION

MV-NY

Published simultaneously in Canada by Little, Brown & Company (Canada) Limited

Printed in the United States of America

Cover illustration: T. Taylor Bruce

Library of Congress Cataloging-in-Publication Data

Egger-Bovet, Howard.
  USKids history. Book of the American colonies / written by Howard Egger-Bovet and Marlene Smith-Baranzini ; illustrated by D. J. Simison.
      p.   cm. — (Brown paper school)
  "A Yolla Bolly Press book"
  Includes index.
  Summary: Discusses the reasons Europeans settled in America, the growth of the original colonies, and the reaction to the newcomers of the people already living in the "New World."
  ISBN 0-316-96920-6 (hc)
  ISBN 0-316-22201-1 (pbk)
  1. United States—History—Colonial period, ca. 1600–1775—Juvenile literature. [1. United States—History—Colonial period, ca. 1600–1775.]   I. Smith-Baranzini, Marlene.   II. Simison, D. J., ill.   III. Title.   IV. Series.
E188.E28   1996
973.2—dc20   95-50456
[973.2]
  10 9 8 7 6 5 4 3 2

Contents

Note: Activities and games are italicized.

Two Boys and a Cow

On the cover of this book is a picture of two boys on a busy dock. Their story begins on page 50. Both boys are immigrants. One came with his family from Brazil. The other one came from England to the Massachusetts Bay Colony in what is now Boston. But soon that family moved again, this time to the Rhode Island Colony where the boy met his friend from Brazil.

The two boys are colonists. They have come from far away to start a new life in America. In our story, each tells the other about himself. Aaron tells Matthew about the parrots in Brazil. Matthew shows Aaron how he orders meat for his family from the butcher on the dock. Soon they will be good friends.

If you look back far enough in your own history you will probably discover that your people came to this country from France, Italy, England, Germany, Ireland, or any number of other places. If they arrived here before this land became a country, they were colonists. The American colonies were settled by immigrants who built their farms and their towns, and eventually formed a government and created the United States of America.

This book is the story of the Europeans who first sailed to this country and explored it. It is the story of the Europeans and others who later came here to settle and make their living in this new land. And it is the story of the Native Americans who already lived here, who met the settlers when they arrived, sometimes saved their lives in difficult times, and sometimes fought them over territory.

The Summer of 1001

They carried their hammocks ashore and put up shelters.

Sailors and Raiders

The people of ancient Scandinavia called themselves Norsemen. They were farmers, craftsmen, merchants, fishermen, and explorers. Some Norsemen took to their wooden sailing ships and roamed the Atlantic waters, raiding other ships. These Scandinavian pirates, who grew wealthy by killing and stealing the riches of others, were called Vikings. Others, like Eirik the Red and his sons, explored the ocean in search of new lands to settle. They were peaceful Norsemen, not Vikings.

Many people believe that the English or the Spanish were the first Europeans to make the voyage across the Atlantic Ocean to America. But rugged Norsemen traveled to this continent more than 400 years before English and Spanish sea captains set their sails to the wind in search of new lands. Leif Eiriksson, a sailor from Greenland, was the first European to set foot on lands that are now in eastern Canada. He carried on a family tradition established by his grandfather and his father, Eirik the Red. When Leif returned home from his voyage to the unknown lands west of Greenland, his ship was loaded with unusual cargo, and he had many tales to tell. The people responded by naming him Leif the Lucky.

On that voyage, Leif had roughly followed the route of another Norseman, Bjarni Herjolfsson, who had reported seeing several new lands west of Greenland. Bjarni was criticized for not stopping to explore them. Some time later, Leif bought Bjarni's ship and gathered a crew of thirty-five men who would explore with him. He asked his father to be their leader. At first, Eirik the Red agreed. But he changed his mind after he was thrown from his horse and injured his leg. The Norsemen believed a fall from a horse was an omen, a sign that something worse might happen. Eirik told his son to sail without him.

After several days of sailing west, Leif and his men sighted land. When they neared it, they anchored their ship. They lowered a small boat over the side and rowed to shore. They called this land Helluland, or "Slab-land," for the huge slabs of rock that stood between the shore and the glaciers. Without stopping for long, they sailed away again, to a flat land with forests and a white sandy beach that met the sea. This land they called Markland, which meant "Forest-land." Most historians think Eirik and his sailors landed first at what is now Baffin Island and then at Labrador, on the continent of North America. Their next stop was at a place they called Vinland, which we think is probably present-day Newfoundland, Canada, in North America.

As far as we know, Leif's voyages were first written about in the thirteenth century, more than 200 years after they took place. We find the story in two old Norse family history accounts. One, named to honor Leif's father, is called *The Saga of Eirik the Red*. History experts think the other one, *The Greenlander's Saga*, is probably more accurate in its details about Leif Eiriksson's journey. Together these sagas provide our first written reports of the Norse exploration of North America.

This is how *The Greenlander's Saga* describes Leif Eiriksson's journey to Vinland in the summer of 1001, after he and his sailors left Helluland and Markland.

"They hurried back to their ship as quickly as possible and sailed away to sea in a northeast wind for two days until they sighted land again. . . . They carried their hammocks ashore and put up booths [stone and turf shelters]. Then they decided to winter there, and built some large houses."

Leif and his men made several surprising discoveries on this land. They found a river and a lake where they caught the largest salmon they had ever seen. Coming from Greenland, they were astounded that even on the shortest day of the year, there were still six hours of daylight.

They formed two parties to explore the country. One of the men returned in excitement. He had found vines and grapes. There were no such berries in Iceland or Greenland, but he had been born in Germany, and he knew what they were.

"They slept for the rest of the night, and the next morning Leif said to his men, 'Now we have two tasks on our hands. On alternate days we must gather grapes and cut vines, and then fell trees, to make a cargo for my ship.'

"This was done. It is said that the towboat was filled with grapes. They took on a full cargo of timber; and in the spring they made ready to leave and sailed away. Leif named the country after its natural qualities and called it *Vinland*."

Sailing back to Greenland, they caught sight of a reef with other Norsemen on it. They anchored and put out a small boat. Leif offered to take the fifteen shipwrecked men aboard. "From then on he was called Leif the Lucky. He gained greatly in wealth and reputation."

They took the shipwrecked men aboard.

A Sturdy Ship

keel

rudder

oar holes

cargo hold

strakes

The remains of several ancient Viking and Norse ships have been discovered in North America over the past one hundred years. Scientists date some of the earliest finds to the ninth and eleventh centuries—close enough to the lifetime of Eirik the Red and Leif Eiriksson to tell us something about the ships they probably sailed.

Every Norse ship was one of a kind, but all shared certain features. Those that were built to travel across oceans were deep and wide and powered by both sails and oars.

The ship Leif bought from Bjarni and sailed to North America was wooden. Oak was the most common building material for Norse ships, but ash, beech, alder, birch, willow, and pine were also used. Eiriksson's ship was built with a rounded bottom and flared sides, designed so it could get close to shore without running aground. It was designed for cargo rather than for speed.

Long overlapping planks, or strakes, ran the length of the ship. Curved floor ribs, or cross-timbers, were regularly spaced to support and reinforce the long planks. The Norsemen caulked, or sealed, the strakes with a paste of animal fur and pine tar to prevent leaks.

A tall center mast, probably made of wood, supported the sail, which could be lowered when oars were needed or as the ship neared land. Iron nails and an iron anchor were also standard equipment. Norse and Viking ships were identified, too, by the single side rudder, necessary for maneuvering through water. Shaped like a long oar, the rudder was fastened with rope to the starboard side, or front left quarter of the ship.

No one knows exactly how long Leif's ship was. Based on the sizes of the Norse ships that have been excavated and the number of oarports on each of their sides, it is likely that Leif's ship was somewhere between sixty and eighty feet long. Sailors slept in the open on long voyages, wherever they could find room, perhaps huddled in pairs for warmth inside animal-skin sleeping bags.

CARVED IVORY AND WHITE FALCONS

On a voyage home from Norway, Leif Eiriksson ran into trouble at sea. Winds drove his ship off course. He was forced to stop at the Hebrides and wait for better weather. The delay wasn't all bad, for Leif fell in love with a young woman named Thorgunna. She wanted to go home with him, but he knew her family would disapprove because he was a foreigner.

Before Leif left the island, he gave Thorgunna three gifts as tokens of his affection for her. These gifts were a gold ring, a woolen cloak made in Greenland, and a belt carved of ivory.

It is not certain how Leif happened to possess a gold ring. The cloak and the belt, however, were typical of Norse handiwork. The women of Greenland cut wool from their sheep to weave warm dresses and hooded wraps. During the long winter nights, the men carved walrus tusks into objects. They designed sets of ivory chessmen to trade or give to others.

More prized than ivory among Norsemen was the white falcon. Hunters sought the majestic bird as a symbol of their own greatness, or to present to royalty when they traveled.

THE SAGA OF EIRIK THE RED

Greenland, the world's largest island, was discovered by Leif Eiriksson's father, Eirik Torvaldson, who was better known as Eirik the Red, for the color of his hair. Eirik was born in Norway. His countrymen banished him to Iceland for three years after Eirik committed a murder.

During his three years of exile, he sailed west from Iceland until he sighted land. He saw that much of it was glacier ice, but he named it "Greenland" anyway, so other people would think it a fine place to go. The trick worked. When his banishment ended, twenty-five ships of Icelandic families and farm animals sailed away with him to settle Greenland.

Only twelve or fourteen ships completed the 200-mile journey in 986 from Iceland to Greenland.

The 450 settlers built their farms in two main areas on the southern end of the island. They built small homes of stone and sod. They ate beef, cheese, and butter from their farms, and hunted bear and caribou.

Maybe you've read about Eirik the Red before, but his name was spelled Erik or Eric. However you spell it, it's the same Eirik. But why so many spellings for one Norseman's name?

Eirik is the spelling we find in the original saga, so it's the most authentic, or genuine, and the one history experts use. *Erik* and *Eric* are modern versions of Eirik.

A few other spellings in this book will look unusual, too, but they really aren't mistakes. They're words you probably know, but like *Eirik*, you're seeing an older version of them.

To help you with these "word mysteries," the modern word appears in brackets beside the old one. But where old and new spellings are nearly identical, we kept the old one to show you how it looked more than 300 years ago.

He gave Thorgunna three gifts.

Write a Family Saga

Before history was written down, it was kept alive through storytelling. Grandparents and parents told their children stories about their ancestors, and these stories were passed from one generation to another. By the twelfth century, people in Iceland and Norway began writing down the accomplishments of family members. These accounts, sometimes written in verse form, were called sagas. Saga writing reached its peak during the twelfth and thirteenth centuries.

Like literature, a saga was meant to be a good story of how people handled life's problems. The storyteller would make it as interesting and creative as he or she wished, even if that meant changing the facts. People didn't expect sagas to be entirely accurate.

You don't have to be an Icelander to write a saga. Find out about the important events in your grandparents' and parents' lives, and write a story about where they were born, the places they have been, and some of the things they did along the way. Try writing it in poetry. Make a cover for your family saga, and decorate it with drawings illustrating your story.

Pages from a Gromet's Diary

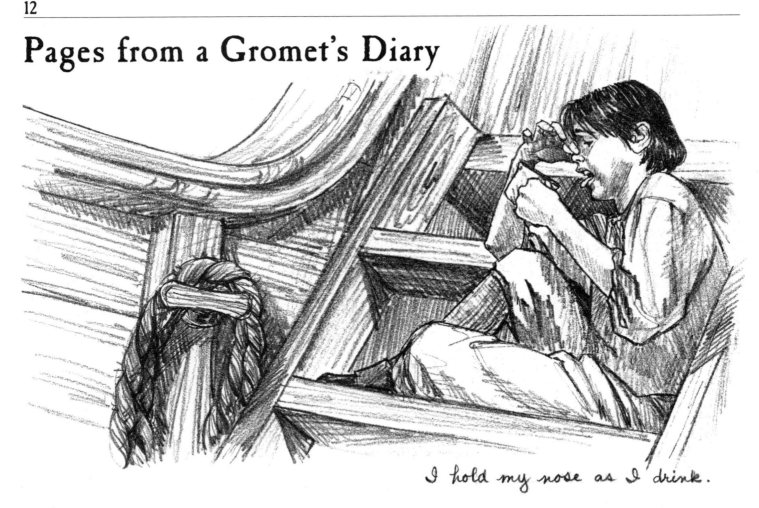

I hold my nose as I drink.

In his youth, Christopher Columbus read a book titled Description of the World, which was written by Marco Polo. The book described Marco Polo's overland travels to the continent of Asia, including the treasures found by this adventurous visitor.

The book captivated Columbus. He was determined to find a sea route to this wondrous land. In 1492 he set out by sailing west from Spain, across the Atlantic Ocean, to find a passageway to Asia. No one had attempted this before. Columbus was confident that the journey wouldn't take long. He believed Asia was much closer to Europe than it actually is.

After ten weeks, an unknown island was finally sighted. Columbus believed this island was located off the Asian coast, near India. He called the people

May 9, 1502   We have set sail! May God hear the prayers we have said and return us safely to Spain.

What luck! I am on the flagship *La Capitana*. We are the lead ship. The other three ships follow us. As well they should. For on this ship is Admiral Columbus.

I have seen little of him. I have been below helping sort supplies. I have seen kidney beans, salted fish, dried fruit, vinegar, oil, and honey. I have told other gromets. Everyone is interested in what will fill their stomachs on this long voyage.

May 15, 1502   I am on the first crew. My duties on deck begin at 3 A.M.—in the dark! The main deck is crowded. I cannot help tripping over the hatches, or being knocked into barrels and spare anchors by the rough seas.

The dark scares me. I fear the dragons. I have heard they live in deep water and will rise up and swallow us.

At 7 A.M. our watch ends. I eat a biscuit, in which I find a bug, and hold my nose as I drink the foul-smelling water. The garlic clove is most satisfying. I find some rolled rope on the deck and lie down to sleep.

May 26, 1502   "West and by south," says Admiral Columbus. This will bring us to the island of Martinique. Glorious! I get to wash my clothes—and myself!

Early August, 1502   We leave the island of Bonacca. I won't forget the Indians. Their canoe was long and held many people. It wasn't difficult to capture it. The Indians carried copper hatchets—and fine beer. We kept their leader to help us speak with other Indians we met.

September 9, 1502   When will it end? It has stormed for weeks. I cannot remember what it is like to wear dry clothes or to taste a hot meal.

We cannot head straight into the wind. Instead, we go forward, making little turns right and left. I work ropes that allow one sail to turn direction.

The order is given to turn starboard. I loosen the rope and pray my rope-burned hands don't get caught in its grasp. The sail flaps furiously. The noise it makes!

I race to the other side and tighten another rope. Now the sail is positioned to move us to port. No sooner have I finished, than the order is given to tack to starboard again.

Back and forth I go. I never stop. Neither does the wind and the rain. The ship collides with the water. Seawater smashes into the boat and floods the deck.

We suffer so. And what makes the suffering so deep is knowing that if we left this horrid coastline for the open sea we would find good weather and fair winds.

There is peace, but not for us. Admiral Columbus will not leave the coast. He is searching for a passage that will lead us to Asia.

Eating a moldy biscuit and some oil and vinegar offers little comfort. I fall asleep wet, covered in salt and bitten by hungry mosquitoes, listening to the crew praying aloud.

October 16, 1502 I have heard no more about finding a passage to Asia, only finding gold.

April 5, 1503 It has been months since my last entry. Much has gone on, but I have been sick and unable to write. We have found a river and gold! We have also found misery. The water level has dropped so much that our ships are stuck in the mud. Indians want to kill us all! Admiral Columbus is crazy with fever.

April 23, 1503 Toredos [shipworms]!

They're eating our ships. There is nothing we can do to stop them. I work the water pump as fast as I can, but it's no use. The water I remove from below comes right back in. The crew is deeply unhappy. We are doomed!

June 25, 1503 We are marooned on Jamaica. Our rotting ships are now moored houses!

July 7, 1503 In two canoes, Admiral Columbus sent Diego Méndez, Bartolomo Fieschi, and sixteen others bound for Spanish land over a hundred miles away. I pray for their safety and our speedy rescue.

January 2, 1504 Mutiny! Why not? There is no sweetness in the New Year. There is no news of rescue. Why not take the canoes and try rescuing ourselves? I want to go with them, but I am weak with fever. I wish them well.

March, 1504 After eight months, a ship has finally come, but not to rescue us. The captain tells us a ship will be sent soon. He leaves us two casks of wine and a slab of pork, then departs.

June 28, 1504 We are saved! Diego Méndez has arrived with a ship. We are bound for the port of Santo Domingo in Hispaniola [now called the Dominican Republic]. I have suffered much for someone so young. I pray God will have mercy on me the rest of my life.

he met Indians. In truth, the island was located off the coast of North America.

Most people are familiar with Columbus's first journey. But he took part in three other voyages, trying each time to find a passage to Asia.

On May 9, 1502, he set sail with a crew of 150 on his fourth and final voyage. Fifty-seven of his crew members were twelve- and thirteen-year-olds. They were called "gromets."

It isn't known if a gromet wrote a diary of Columbus's fourth, and most dangerous, voyage. But if one had, the following might be what that diary would have contained.

I race to the other side.

COLUMBUS,
A MAN OF HIS TIME

You are a product of your times. You cannot escape this fact. Your ideas and your beliefs are shaped by what you see and hear all your life. The same was true for Christopher Columbus. He was a product of the 1400s.

The 1400s forced the captain of a ship to sharpen his senses or be doomed to failure, because few precise navigational instruments existed at that time.

Columbus was one of the finest ship commanders of his time. He developed the ability to discover vital information from the wind, the sea, and the stars. Such skills allowed him to find inhabited lands that Europeans never knew existed.

Columbus also lived during a time when slavery was acceptable. Even the Catholic Church approved of this practice.

Columbus enslaved Indians to find gold. Many were tortured and murdered. If Columbus acted this way today, his actions would be condemned. He would stand trial for murder and other crimes.

In the 1400s, however, he was not regarded as a criminal. To many people Columbus was a superb sailor and explorer.

Why Leave Home?

Why did explorers sail dangerous seas to unknown lands? For adventure? Yes, but there were other, more practical reasons, too.

Europeans wanted the goods of Asia: gold, silk, spices, and jewels. They could get these goods from Venetian and other European merchants. These merchants controlled the land routes to Asia. They commanded high prices for their goods. They had good reason to.

Merchants were constantly in danger as they traveled back and forth to Asia. There was always a tough mountain pass to cross, or a thief waiting to rob you.

Other European nations didn't care about the dangers merchants faced. They were tired of making merchants wealthy. Nations like Portugal, Spain, and Holland decided to make themselves wealthy by finding sea routes to Asia.

TIME IN A BOTTLE

There were no clocks on board Columbus's ships. To tell time the sailors used a device just like an hourglass, only it was a "half-hourglass." The sand would take approximately a half hour to empty out of one glass into another.

A boy was in charge of turning over the glass every half hour. As the sand ran out of one chamber, the boy would call out, "One glass is gone and now the second floweth," or, "Four glasses have gone and now the fifth floweth."

The crew paid special attention to these announcements. With each half-hour call it meant one group of sailors' work was that much closer to ending, and the other group's shift was that much closer to starting.

Each shift was four hours. However, to shorten the work shift, the boy sometimes turned the half-hourglass over before the sand emptied out of a chamber.

When a group's shift was a half hour from ending, the boy turned over the half-hourglass for the eighth time and recited: "Good is that which has past, better that which shall come; seven is past and eight floweth, more shall flow if God wills; count and pass make the voyage fast."

THE TIMES WERE CHANGING

Columbus lived during a time of great change. The years between A.D. 450 and the 1400s were called the Middle Ages. During this time, there were no forceful kings to prevent wars.

Many Europeans were afraid. They took comfort in the church. They abandoned exploration, new ideas in science and mathematics, and knowledge gathered by the Greeks and Romans.

Eventually, times changed. Trade brought prosperity to people. Cities grew. Once again scholars became interested in learning about the mathematics and philosophy of the Greeks and Romans. There was renewed interest in new ideas and exploration.

Inventions that had been ignored were now accepted. The decimal system began to be used. A wheeled plow pulled by a horse replaced the crude plow pulled by an ox. And new inventions, such as the compass and the printing press, were created.

This new era was called the Renaissance, or the Modern Age. It was a time of great thinking and exploration. The Renaissance helped shape the world we live in today.

Make a Compass

A compass has the ability to tell which direction is north. This is possible because the compass needle is magnetized. This magnetized needle is attracted to the magnetic pull of the North Pole. A compass needle always points to magnetic north. The other side of the needle always points to magnetic south.

Columbus and other explorers were aware that there were two different sets of North and South Poles. There were the *magnetic* north and south poles and the *geographic* North and South Poles.

Columbus knew the magnetic and geographic poles were in different locations. Columbus used the North Star to correct his ship's direction.

The compass may not be perfect, but in Columbus's time it was invaluable in determining a northerly direction when at sea. Many times the sky was cloudy. Without being able to see the sun or the stars, the compass was the only navigational tool a sailor could rely on.

Here's how to make your own compass.

You Will Need:

A common pin, a magnet, a cork, glue, a bowl, and some water.

1. Magnetize the pin by rubbing it against the magnet.
2. Glue the pin to the cork.
3. Pour some water into the bowl.
4. Place the cork in the water. Notice how the cork begins to move. The pin is attracted to the magnetic pull of the North and South Poles.
5. Move the bowl. The needle still points toward the *magnetic* north and south poles.

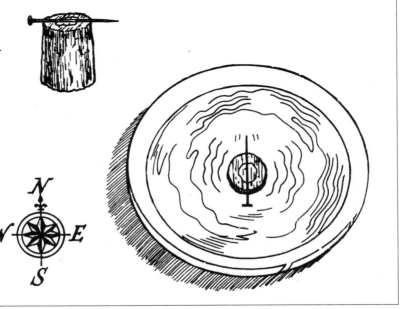

Have a Bland Day

In the 1400s spices were difficult to obtain and could be expensive. Even so, everyone wanted to put spices in their food. But it wasn't necessarily for flavor.

There was no refrigeration in the 1400s. Meat, fish, and vegetables spoiled quickly. But people couldn't afford to throw away spoiled food.

Spices were the answer. Spice helped cover the smell of rotting ingredients. Most people used pepper because of its strong taste. It was also inexpensive, as was salt, which was used to preserve meats and fishes. The wealthy could afford other spices, such as saffron and cinnamon.

Today many spices are available and affordable. But what if salt and pepper were the only daily spices most people used?

For a day, eliminate all foods that have any spice, except salt and pepper. Remember to check food labels, and ask your parents what spices are in the meals they've prepared.

Having a bland day will give you an appreciation of the plentiful variety of spices we have today.

The next time you're in a grocery store, check out the spices that are available, and see how much each one costs. Which spice is the most expensive?

The First Explorers

(A) Vikings 1000
The Vikings were the first people from the European continent to reach the North American coast.

(B 1,2) Cabot 1498
John Cabot, an Italian explorer, was hired by the English king to explore the New England coast. He made two trips, claiming England's first territory in North America.

(C) Balboa 1513
Spanish explorer Vasco Núñez de Balboa was the first European to see the Pacific Ocean.

Cortés 1519
Spaniard Hernando Cortés explored the land of the Aztecs, today called Mexico.

(E) Magellan 1519
Ferdinand Magellan, a Spaniard, was the first European to sail around the world.

(F) Cartier 1534
Jacques Cartier, a French explorer, surveyed the land that would later become Canada.

(G) Hudson 1610
Henry Hudson, an English navigator hired by the Dutch, claimed land that was to become the first Dutch colony in North America.

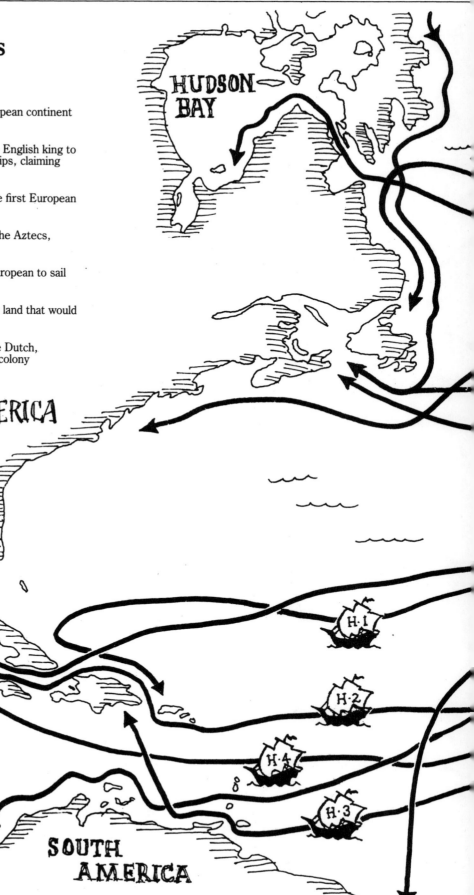

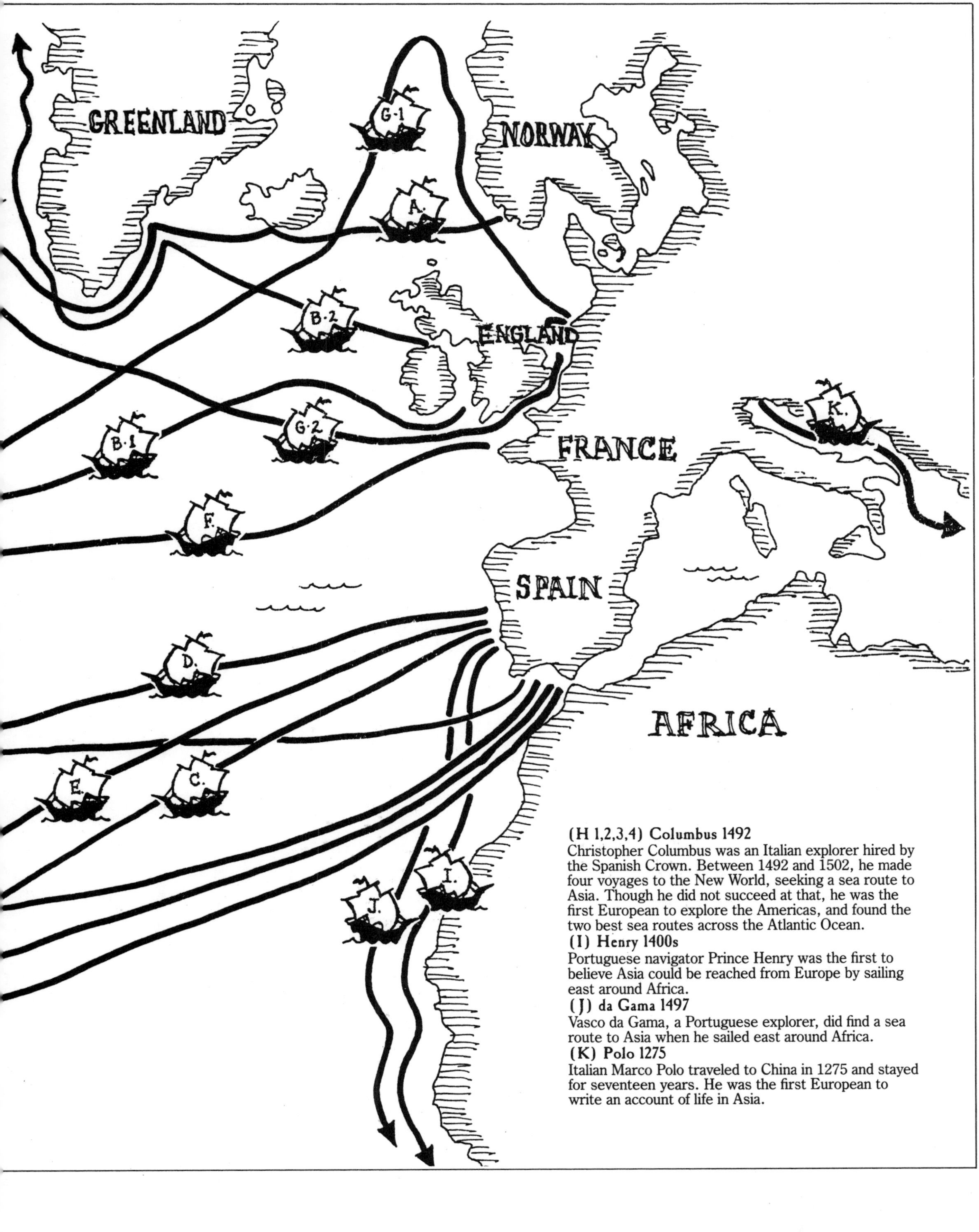

GREENLAND

NORWAY

G·1

A.

B·2

ENGLAND

B·1

G·2

K.

F.

FRANCE

D.

SPAIN

E.

C.

AFRICA

J.

I.

(H 1,2,3,4) Columbus 1492
Christopher Columbus was an Italian explorer hired by
the Spanish Crown. Between 1492 and 1502, he made
four voyages to the New World, seeking a sea route to
Asia. Though he did not succeed at that, he was the
first European to explore the Americas, and found the
two best sea routes across the Atlantic Ocean.

(I) Henry 1400s
Portuguese navigator Prince Henry was the first to
believe Asia could be reached from Europe by sailing
east around Africa.

(J) da Gama 1497
Vasco da Gama, a Portuguese explorer, did find a sea
route to Asia when he sailed east around Africa.

(K) Polo 1275
Italian Marco Polo traveled to China in 1275 and stayed
for seventeen years. He was the first European to
write an account of life in Asia.

The Captain's Decision

Captain Lane lay still, listening to the wind.

The Englishmen in the Roanoke Island stories in this section—men like Captain Ralph Lane, Sir Francis Drake, and others—do not appear on the map of explorers in this book. That's because after new lands were sighted, many years passed before colonists made preparations to survive so far from home.

Lane and Drake did not sail until the late sixteenth century, when England wanted to try colonizing the New World (America). It did not matter that Spain—thanks to sailors like Christopher Columbus—had already claimed the New World.

Sir Walter Raleigh organized the first English colony to go to America. He placed Captain Ralph Lane in charge of the colonists who landed at Roanoke Island in 1586. That summer, Lane sent his report of the colony's plight and Sir Drake's rescue to Sir Raleigh in London. No one can say exactly how Captain Lane felt when he decided to leave America, but we can guess that he was disappointed and concerned about his decision. This story is based on his report. Some details have been added.

Captain Lane blew out the candle. He lay still, listening to the wind roar through the treetops. Hailstones pounded against the rough shelter and rainwater poured in under the door. The house groaned, as if the storm might rip it apart. Lane huddled in fear. Should he flee for the safety of Fort Raleigh, or would he only lose his way in the storm? Somewhere near the house a tree trunk snapped. He decided to stay put.

Lying in the darkness, he worried about his colonists. Most of them would be safe in their two-story homes near the fort. But some of his best officers were aboard ship in the fleet commanded by Sir Francis Drake. Their lives were in grave danger. Whatever a hurricane might do on land, its force at sea was ten times mightier. Lane prayed for them.

The colonists remained inside and waited out the storm. It raged for three days and three nights. One sailor said it brought "thunder . . . and raigne with hailstones as Bigge as hennes egges." It created "great Spowtes at the seas as thoughe heaven & [earth] would . . . [meet]."

On June 16, 1586, the storm eased. Sir Francis Drake came ashore in a small boat. Lane met him. They walked to the fort. Instead of the good cheer that accompanied their earlier talks, the men were sober. In a lifetime at sea, Drake said, never had he witnessed such a hurricane. Both men were rethinking their agreement.

Just one week ago, Drake and his fleet of twenty-three ships had sailed into sight of the struggling colony. The colonists had been hoping desperately for an English supply ship that was three months late. Instead, they celebrated Sir Francis Drake's arrival. Rumors of his cargo—most of it boldly stolen from Spanish ships—spread through the fort. Before long, the weary colonists were drinking Spanish wine and eating fresh fish.

Drake and Lane had talked for hours. Drake, the mightiest sea captain ever to sail for England, had come north to check on the queen's first colony in America. Instead of a thriving settlement, he found men weakened by hunger, out of gunpowder, and without a ship in their harbor.

Like Captain Lane, Drake wanted this colony to succeed. He would give Lane one of his best ships, several small boats, a healthy crew, and food and supplies to last a month. Drake would provide another ship that would sail the weakest colonists back to England.

But now Lane listened to Drake's report of the hurricane's destruction. Anchor lines had strained and split on the wild seas. Several of Drake's ships had vanished, including the *Francis*, with Lane's officers aboard. Suddenly Drake was not much better off than the colonists.

Lane faced an important decision. The storm had left his colonists more discouraged than ever. The supply ship might still arrive. He could wait for it. But now the colonists had a chance to return to England. Should they abandon the colony they had tried so hard to establish?

Drake was anxious to leave the dangerous coast as soon as possible. Lane gathered his men, "such Captaines and Gentlemen of my companie as then were at hand." They seem to have agreed: they hoped to leave. Lane prepared a document. He said the final decision had been made by the Almighty. He made a list of his reasons for leaving, signed it, and delivered it to Drake.

Small boats quickly gathered the colonists and their belongings. But the boats were too heavy. The sailors threw overboard "all our Cardes, Bookes and writings." Many of John White's drawings of the colony were lost. Three men, away from the fort during the storm, had not returned. But the weather was still stormy. The fleet would not wait.

On June 18 Drake's damaged fleet, with all but the three missing colonists, set sail for England. It stopped along the coast of Newfoundland, where Drake knew they could get fresh fish and water before making the long voyage across the Atlantic Ocean. Four weeks after they left Roanoke Island, the colonists landed safely in Portsmouth, England.

The sailors threw overboard "all our writings."

Two Algonquin Indians arrived at the palace.

Ten Tough Colony Questions

If you could start a colony like Sir Walter Raleigh did on Roanoke Island, would you want to? Do you know of places in the world that aren't populated? (There are some. Check an atlas for maps and population figures.) Where would you like to go, and who would you take with you? Would you go someplace far away, like the colonists did, knowing you might never return to your homeland again? If your belongings had to fit into a small suitcase, what would you choose?

What is the farthest distance you have already gone from home? Who in your family has traveled the farthest? When your family is having dinner or riding in the car together, ask them one or two of these questions. Their answers might surprise you.

TO CONVINCE THE QUEEN

When Raleigh's English explorers anchored their two ships and went ashore in the New World in 1584, they quickly announced that they were the new owners of everything they saw. Without pausing to consider the Algonquin Indians—already quite at home on the land—the newcomers claimed it theirs, "in the name of God and Queen Elizabeth."

The queen of England was a well-educated woman, interested in everything around her. She might have liked to see the New World, but in her time a queen could not risk the danger of ocean travel. She was delighted when explorers brought her treasures from their journeys. She was probably surprised, though, when two Algonquin Indians arrived at the palace.

The Indians (today we call them "Algonquian") were part of Walter Raleigh's plan to convince Queen Elizabeth that owning colonies in America would make England stronger and richer than Spain. Elizabeth favored anything that would weaken Spain. The Algonquin could provide new products for English trade. If the Indians could be converted to Protestantism, the Spanish king, who was Catholic, would be even more frustrated.

The queen agreed to help with the colony.

She made the handsome and ambitious Raleigh a knight. She appointed him the lord and governor of the colony, and allowed him to change the Indian name of the land, Wingandacon, to Virginia, in her honor. The new name was considered a compliment, because Elizabeth I, who had never married, was known as "the Virgin Queen." Sir Walter Raleigh also received ammunition from the royal supply and his flagship—the ship that flies the nation's flag and leads the fleet.

Later in his lifetime, Raleigh explored South America and wrote a book about his adventures. He helped the new English colonies by introducing tobacco and potatoes into Ireland. He remained a favorite of Elizabeth I until he upset her by secretly marrying Elizabeth Throckmorton, a young palace maid who served the queen.

When Queen Elizabeth died, Raleigh faced many difficulties. King James I didn't trust him and had him thrown into prison in the Tower of London. During the thirteen years that he was kept there, his wife and son were allowed to visit him, as were many famous poets and great scholars.

In 1616 Sir Walter Raleigh was freed by the king and allowed to search for gold in South America. Before he left England, he was given orders not to fight with the Spanish. But Raleigh disobeyed, and in 1618 he was put to death.

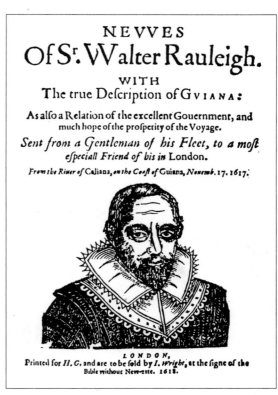

NEVVES
Of Sr. Walter Rauleigh.
WITH
The true Description of GVIANA:
As also a Relation of the excellent Gouernment, and much hope of the prosperity of the Voyage.
Sent from a Gentleman of his Fleet, to a most especiall Friend of his in London.
From the River of Caliana, on the Coast of Guiana, Nouemb. 17. 1617.

LONDON,
Printed for H. G. and are to be sold by I. Wright, at the signe of the Bible without New-gate. 1618.

MANTEO AND WANCHESE, ALGONQUIN INTERPRETERS

In 1584 it was not unusual for Indians to meet new people. Dozens of different tribes lived along the Atlantic Coast, around bays, and in the woodlands beyond. Trade relationships often brought them together. They learned to speak each other's languages and formed new bonds through ties of marriage. Sometimes two or three chiefs united their people to stop an enemy tribe from overstepping its rights.

In some ways, then, the pale-skinned men sent by Sir Walter Raleigh to settle in the New World were simply strangers from another "tribe." The Native Americans welcomed Captain Philip Amadas, Captain Arthur Barlowe, and the other heavily dressed Englishmen who came ashore, and invited them to supper in their small Indian village of cedar bark homes. One of the English sailors who was there said the bare-chested Roanoke were "very handsome and goodly people" who wore shell jewelry and animal skins.

Manteo and Wanchese, two young men from different Algonquin tribes, were as curious about English life as the Englishmen were about them. Manteo and Wanchese liked the captains' idea that they could live in London for a year and learn to speak English. In an arrangement something like today's "exchange students," who study in foreign countries, Manteo and Wanchese moved to England that summer.

Their arrival in London created much excitement, and it convinced Sir Walter Raleigh to send colonists to live near Roanoke. Unfortunately, we do not know what the young Algonquin Indians thought of their experiences in England. Most accounts say they spent a pleasant year there, acting as interpreters.

Manteo, a popular, likable fellow, adopted many English habits. When he returned home a year later, with the first Roanoke colonists, he played an important part in keeping the English and Indians on good terms. Wanchese, on the other hand, grew to dislike and distrust the English. Some people thought he was jealous of Manteo for being more popular. Others believed he could see more clearly that the English planned someday to overpower the Indians and take their lands.

The Native Americans invited them to supper.

The Lost Colony

The Spanish Armada

During the first half of the sixteenth century, Spain enjoyed being the strongest country in Europe. But when Queen Elizabeth of England rose to the throne in 1558, she encouraged her sea captains to stir up trouble with Spain on the oceans.

For one thing, her father, Henry VIII, had broken away from the Roman Catholic Church and named himself as head of the Church of England. His action turned Spain, a Catholic nation, into England's bitter enemy. At the same time, England was growing stronger.

In 1588 King Philip of Spain became fed up with England's constant sea attacks. He sent an armada, or a fleet of Spanish warships, to the English Channel to fight back. But the English were waiting for them in newer and faster ships, and defeated the armada. Smaller sea battles continued for several years and colonial exploration nearly stood still. When the fighting finally stopped, England was declared ruler of the seas.

Some of the men who left Roanoke with Sir Francis Drake in 1586 wanted to try colonizing North America again. John White was one of them. Because he was trustworthy, he was appointed governor of a new settlement in Virginia, to be named Raleigh. He had already made the voyage across the Atlantic twice, first with Captain Amadas in 1584, and then as a colonist with Captain Lane. On both of those trips, John White had painted and sketched the plants, animals, and people of the New World.

In April 1587, White and about 120 people sailed to the New World from Portsmouth, England, in three ships. This time, the colonists included fifteen married women, two single women, and nine children.

When they arrived at Roanoke, they found that Fort Raleigh had been destroyed. But the houses built by the first colonists needed only a little repair. The men also built new homes for the families.

Governor White had been disturbed by the mistrust between the first group of colonists and the Indians. Before they left, the first Englishmen had killed the Roanoke Chief Wingina and massacred many tribesmen. Governor White wanted to do things differently this time. He sent messages of friendship to the Croatoan, but for some of the English and the Indians, it was already too late. The colonists acted badly at times. They talked of building trust among the tribes, but they also staged surprise attacks against the Indians.

Chief Manteo told his people to forgive those few Englishmen and make peace with the others. But many Croatoan Indians could not forget what the colonists had done.

That summer, someone from the colony needed to go to England for more supplies. When no one else would go, White agreed to make the trip. It was probably a poor decision, not only because he left the colony without a leader, but also because he was one of the few colonists who got along well with the Indians.

The colonists formed a plan so that White could find them when he returned. If they moved, they would carve on a tree the name of where they went. If they left in trouble, they would mark the sign of the cross.

Before Governor White left Roanoke, he packed his paintings and art supplies in a chest, to keep them safe until he returned. He had good news to take to England. Chief Manteo had been baptized in the Christian faith. A new baby had just been born in the colony. White's daughter, Eleanor, and her husband, Ananias Dare, celebrated the birth of a daughter. In honor of Queen Elizabeth and the new colony, they named their baby Virginia.

So many problems arose for John White in England that two years passed before Sir Raleigh could finally send another fleet to Roanoke. The ships arrived on August 15. John White, who had waited through all the delays, was full of hope. He wrote in his diary that night, "At our first comming to anker [anchor] on this shore, we saw a great smoke rise in the Ile Raonoak neere the place where I left our Colony in the yeere 1587, which smoake put us in good hope that some of the Colony were there expecting my returne out of England." He, too, looked forward to seeing his family. His grandchild Virginia was two years old already.

But when the men finally reached Roanoke, the island was deserted. A wall of timber surrounded the houses. Iron tools, covered by overgrown grass and weeds, were scattered about. Several trunks that had once been buried were found opened and their contents spread everywhere. White's artwork was ruined and his books torn apart.

Carved on a tree outside the wall White found the letters C R O. Near the houses, on a tree stripped of its bark, was the word *Croatoan*.

White hoped this clue would lead to his family and the other colonists.

The men sailed south toward the Croatoan village and anchored for the night. A coastal storm rose and winds snapped the ships' cables one by one. The ships escaped to deep water. In the morning the men agreed the search had become too dangerous. Reluctantly, they sailed through the storm, making their way toward England. They had seen no sign of the colonists.

Explanations for the disappearance of the lost colonists of Roanoke Island range from the likely to the improbable. Most historians believe that the colonists died, some were killed by the Indians, and others joined the Indians and lived with them.

One Indian account says the colonists found their way to the village of a friendly Croatoan tribe, and the baby, Virginia Dare, was adopted by the chief. His wife named her Ulalee, which means wood thrush.

According to this legend, Ulalee grew into a beautiful young woman, with fair hair and violet eyes. She sang the tribal songs with a clear, pure voice. An old medicine man wished to make her his wife. But Ulalee had fallen in love with a handsome young man who loved her deeply. When she refused to marry the medicine man, his magic changed her into a white doe.

Four hundred years after the colonists vanished, people still say a mysterious ghost deer roams the swamps near the old Indian village. They claim that the spirit of Ulalee still lives within the doe.

The island was deserted.

Strange Ships in the Bay

something strange was floating on the water.

The Powhatan boy had seen something strange floating on the water. He described what he saw to the Powhatan chief. The boy mentioned three objects, enormous, bewildering, canoe-like things. The chief had seen them before. They were foreign ships! Word spread quickly.

The chief sent some men down to the shore of the bay. The boy was allowed to join his father. This privilege, along with a shredded copper earring, was his reward from the chief.

By the riverbank, near the bay, the father and his son climbed a tree and looked out at the harbor. There, as his son had described, were three ships.

The news traveled up the river. Men stationed along the riverbank passed the information until it reached the chief. Now it was confirmed. There were intruders in the bay.

The people continued their daily work. But it was impossible to talk about anything but the arrival of the strangers. Every villager listened for further news.

Back by the bay, the boy noticed some men had left the big ship. They were heading toward the river in a smaller vessel. The boy pointed to the smaller craft and signaled the men below, who in turn passed this information on to the chief.

The small vessel passed beneath the boy and his father. Keeping perfectly still, the boy stared at the strangers' odd appearance. Their skin was white, and their faces were not plucked free of hair. The strangers' bodies were completely covered with heavy clothes, even though the weather was warm.

The strangers traveled upriver. When the craft was far enough away, the boy and his father silently climbed down the tree and returned home.

Eventually, the strangers arrived at the village. The chief and his family met the white men. They greeted their guests dressed in their finest clothing. The chief's body was painted all black. On his head he wore black horns. The color black was worn on important occasions. It was the chief's hope that these men would be allies against his enemies.

The strangers and the chief spoke. The white men referred to Powhatan words they carried with them in a book. These words, and their meanings, were brought back to England by previous visitors. When these words were inadequate, they used sign language to understand each other.

The chief invited the men to his bark-covered house for a feast. As they sat on mats, the men were served ample portions of venison and corn bread. Children peeked inside to stare and giggle at their peculiar guests. The boy who had spotted the three ships didn't gawk or giggle. He wondered if the strangers would be friends or enemies.

The white men did not act like enemies. They didn't talk of war. By the time the men left to continue upriver, the boy felt the white men were the Powhatan's friends.

Over a week later, however, the white men returned and anchored by an island in the river near the boy's village. The next day, the three large ships joined the small vessel.

From atop a tree, the boy watched the men unload crates of supplies onto the island. They began building a fort. The white men were not visiting. They were staying!

The boy was troubled by the white men living so close to his village. Why were they here? The boy felt like the deer he had stalked many days ago. Were the white men really friends, or only pretending to be?

The boy watched the men unload supplies.

The Jamestown Brothers

Two officers jumped down and grabbed Jack and Edward.

Jack and Edward begged for money from people entering a London tavern. They stood close to the building to keep away from the cold wind that pierced their tattered clothing.

"Did you notice the fur hats on their heads?" Jack asked his brother, holding a coin in his hand.

"I did," winked Edward. "Those with money are here tonight. And when they come out we'll say, 'I charge you in the name of the king to give me a pound.'"

"No, give me two," laughed Jack.

The street was quiet in front of the tavern. The brothers picked up two sticks and a ball stuffed with hair. They walked out into the street and played. When customers began leaving the tavern, the brothers rushed back to beg for more money.

A cart driven by a king's officer turned the corner. Two officers quickly jumped down and grabbed Jack and Edward. They tossed them inside the cart, which was filled with other homeless children, and drove off.

Jack and Edward believed they had been arrested for begging. Days later they found out the true reason. The brothers and ninety-eight other children were carted to the docks and placed on ships.

"What are you doing with us?" demanded Jack and Edward.

"You're lucky, my sons," answered a man from a local church. "You're being given another chance. The church is sending you to Virginia. Hard work in a new land will be your salvation."

Jack and Edward spent the next four months at sea. They had never been on a ship before. The rough water made them sick, and the crowded conditions made them long for the streets of London.

Finally the ship arrived off the shores of Virginia. One hundred homeless children

The London Company established a colony in Virginia in 1607. In order to succeed, the colony needed laborers to do physical work. The company turned to the streets of London. Homeless people, including many children, crowded the city. Children were abandoned by parents with large families. Other children became homeless when their parents died of disease.

In 1609 homeless adults were sent to Virginia. More fortunate people thought it a good way to rid the city of the poor and give Virginia the help it needed. In 1617 one hundred homeless children were also shipped to Virginia. Were there two brothers among them? We don't know. However, if there were two brothers, this might be their story.

pushed and shoved to get a glimpse of their new home. Jack and Edward looked out at the land. They searched for something familiar, anything that reminded them of London. All they saw were endless trees.

"Where are the streets?" Edward wondered.

"Where is the city?" Jack asked.

Eventually the ship made its way up the James River and anchored off the island of Jamestown. The children were rowed ashore. Waiting to greet them were the settlers. Children anxiously listened as their names were read off and their new families came forward. Jack's name was called. A large bearded man stepped forward to claim him. His clothes were worn and his right arm was injured.

"What about my brother, Edward?" asked Jack.

"He will live with another family," said the man. "But the fort is small; you will see him."

Jack turned toward Edward. Since their parents had passed away, two years ago, they had spent every day together. Jack hadn't counted on being separated from his brother.

"Sir, I must protest," pleaded Jack. "My younger brother, he must come with me. He is only seven years old."

"I understand, but he has already been spoken for," said the man. "You must come with me." The man forcefully led Jack into the fort. Jack could do nothing but look back and stare at his younger brother. Edward stood there crying.

Jack entered the fort. There were thatched houses, a well, and a storehouse. In the fort's center stood a church. The man led Jack into his house. "My name is John Phillips. This is my home, and now it is your home, too."

It had been two years since Jack had a home. He surveyed the living room. There was little in it. Between the beams of the ceiling and the planks of the floor was a chair, several benches, a table, a chest, a gun, and some pots. Jack looked at the glowing fireplace at the far wall. It reminded him of his mother and the many evenings she had spent by the fire mending clothes and spinning wool. Jack thought about Edward again.

There was a knock at the door. John Phillips opened it. There stood a man with Edward, whose eyes were red from crying.

"God keep you, John," said the man. "I brought Edward over to see his brother. I believe he misses him, though it could be London."

"No sir, I miss my brother, Jack," asserted Edward.

"Well, here he is," said John Phillips.

Edward ran into Jack's arms.

"Don't be afraid, Edward, I'm here."

"Edward," said the man. "Let's go now. There's much to be done. You'll see your brother tomorrow in the field."

The man led Edward away. John Phillips sat down at the table. Jack did the same. "This is your home, Jack, whether you like it or not. You'll work hard as God intended you to do, and I'll be a father to you."

"Do you have a wife?" Jack asked.

"She died last year. My only son died the year before that." John Phillips noticed Jack staring at his arm. "My arm was broken by an Indian arrow," revealed John Phillips. "Indians and settlers fight each other, but we are still here. And now, so are you."

The Jamestown Story

The box was opened.

This is the title page for a pamphlet entitled "Nova Britannia." This pamphlet, published in 1609, was an advertisement for settling in Virginia. In the pamphlet the author speaks of Virginia's beauty: "There are valleys and plains streaming with sweet springs, like veins in a natural body." He also states that the colony will not replace the Indians, but "tend to their greater good" and "plant ourselves in their country."

In England many families worked on farms. But in the 1600s English farm life changed. Landowners turned farmland into pastures because there was greater profit in raising cattle and sheep. This change caused a dramatic decrease in farming jobs.

Families were forced to travel about England, looking for work. An enormous increase in the population made it difficult to find a job in the countryside, but there was work in cities like London. But many people flocked to London only to find there were more people than jobs. London streets became a home for the homeless.

In 1606 an event occurred that would change people's lives in London—and all of England. Wealthy merchants formed the London Company and petitioned the king to grant a royal charter to approve the formation of a colony in Virginia. Virginia had an abundance of timber, furs, and the possibility of gold. Virginia offered an opportunity for profit.

With the king's approval, the company created a plan to generate this profit. Settlers would gather valuable cargo and send it back to England. The goods would be sold and the profits would be used to pay investors and send over shiploads of unemployed laborers and craftsmen. These people, called indentured servants, would work seven years for the company, at which time they would be free to create profitable lives for themselves.

On December 20, 1606, three ships traveled the Thames River to the open sea bound for Virginia. The ships carried 144 men and boys, tools, ammunition, weapons, food, and grains. On the flagship, there was a sealed box carrying the settlers' orders. The box was to remain sealed until the ships reached Virginia.

After five months of sea travel, the ships reached the Virginia shore on April 26, 1607. The box was opened. The orders were read. The settlers were to select a site for the colony. This land would be the company's property. They were to take notes on plants and how to treat the Indians, explore the rivers, and gather valuable cargo.

There was one other item in the box: a list of settlers' names to be the colony's ruling council. One name on the list angered the settlers. The name was John Smith. Smith had irritated many people during the voyage by showing his disgust for anyone who complained about the journey.

Smith, at age twenty-seven, was a seasoned soldier. He had fought in many European battles. He knew how to survive in rough conditions. Smith was a born leader, but the colonists and the council spurned Smith instead of enlisting his help.

The council was disorganized. They chose a

poor site for the first colony. The land was swampy. Mosquitoes carrying malaria killed many people. An attack by Powhatan warriors almost finished the colony, but the ships' guns forced an Indian retreat.

If these problems weren't enough, one-third of the colonists were gentlemen. English gentlemen weren't used to physical labor, nor did they want to get used to it. Hard work was for servants. The gentlemen refused to cut wood for housing or plant crops for food.

When autumn came, and food became scarce, John Smith managed to trade for corn with the Indians. Later, while exploring the Chickahominy River, he was captured by Chief Powhatan, the supreme ruler of the Powhatan. Smith was to be executed, but he was saved by Chief Powhatan's daughter, Pocahontas.

Smith and Chief Powhatan became friends. But this friendship couldn't save settlers from starvation. The people's refusal to store food caused many settlers to die. By spring, over half of the people in the colony were dead.

John Smith had had enough of this sniveling attitude. He told the settlers if they didn't work, they didn't eat. Gentlemen settlers were outraged, but with Smith's persistence crops were planted and a fort was built. His friendly relationship with Chief Powhatan prevented Indian attacks.

But not even John Smith could prevent the colony's greatest enemy: fire. In 1608 fire raged through the wooden fort, sending settlers racing for their lives. The fort burned to the ground. Colonists were left defenseless against the Great Frost of 1608. Three huts remained to house 150 people. With Smith's determination, the fort was rebuilt. Soon, more ships arrived to increase the settlement's population.

Smith left James Fort for England in October 1609, satisfied that the colony was well organized. But with his departure chaos returned to Jamestown. That winter was called the "starving time." Indian attacks and a lack of food caused the population to drop from 500 to 60 settlers. People huddled in the fort, surviving by eating rats, insects, and dogs.

In 1611 Thomas Dale was made the colony's governor. He forced the settlers to follow a strict schedule to increase productivity and reduce laziness. His method caused the colony to grow. Still, the London Company wanted to see a profit.

In 1612 John Rolfe discovered that tobacco brought from Trinidad grew well in Virginia. Tobacco soon became the export the company was looking for. Tobacco was sold in Europe for a handsome profit. The company was further helped by problems back in England. Crop failures and bubonic and pneumonic plague killed thousands of people, and many English people, both poor and rich, grew eager to resettle in Virginia.

By 1618 there were eleven settlements in Virginia. The London Company allowed private ownership of land and called for the formation of elected representatives to advise the governor. By 1619 houses were built beyond the forts' walls.

Jamestown was the capital of the Virginia Colony for over ninety years. But during those years, the town had been plagued repeatedly by fires, Indian attacks, and disease. In 1698 the colony's capital was moved to less-dangerous Williamsburg.

Today you can visit a reconstruction of James Fort at Jamestown Festival Park, one mile upriver from the settlement's original location.

Come on Down to Jamestown

What if the London Company commissioned you to create a broadside or an advertisement pamphlet like "Nova Britannia"? What would you do? What information would you include? Should you describe the Virginia landscape? Should you mention the dangers of disease? How about a drawing? What kind of picture would attract a person to move to Virginia? And what about a title for your broadside or pamphlet?

Get out your pencil, paper, and art tools, or sit down at a computer if one is available, and create your best sales pitch. Your broadside or pamphlet can be produced on standard 8½- by 11-inch white paper. In the 1600s paper wasn't white, though, because it wasn't bleached to remove its natural beige color. To give your paper a beige tint, paint your paper with brown watercolor paint or black tea.

Draw several versions of your broadside on scrap paper. When you are satisfied with your work, create a final draft. Use this draft as a guide, and transfer your advertisement to the beige-tinted paper.

If you are creating a pamphlet, fold your paper in half. The front page is your title page. It will include the pamphlet title, a statement telling one of Virginia's advantages (such as good farmland), and a drawing. At the bottom of the title page, write where the pamphlet was produced, who printed it, and the date of printing. The text of your advertisement will be placed on the inside two pages. The back page can be filled with another drawing.

People huddled in the fort.

The Jamestown settlement began as the James Fort, which was named after King James I. The triangular-shaped fort was built on one acre of land and was surrounded and protected by a tall wooden fence. By 1621 the population had grown so large that a town was built beyond the fort. This town was Jamestown.

Plows and spades such as those used in early Jamestown.

paring spade

turving spade

trenching spade

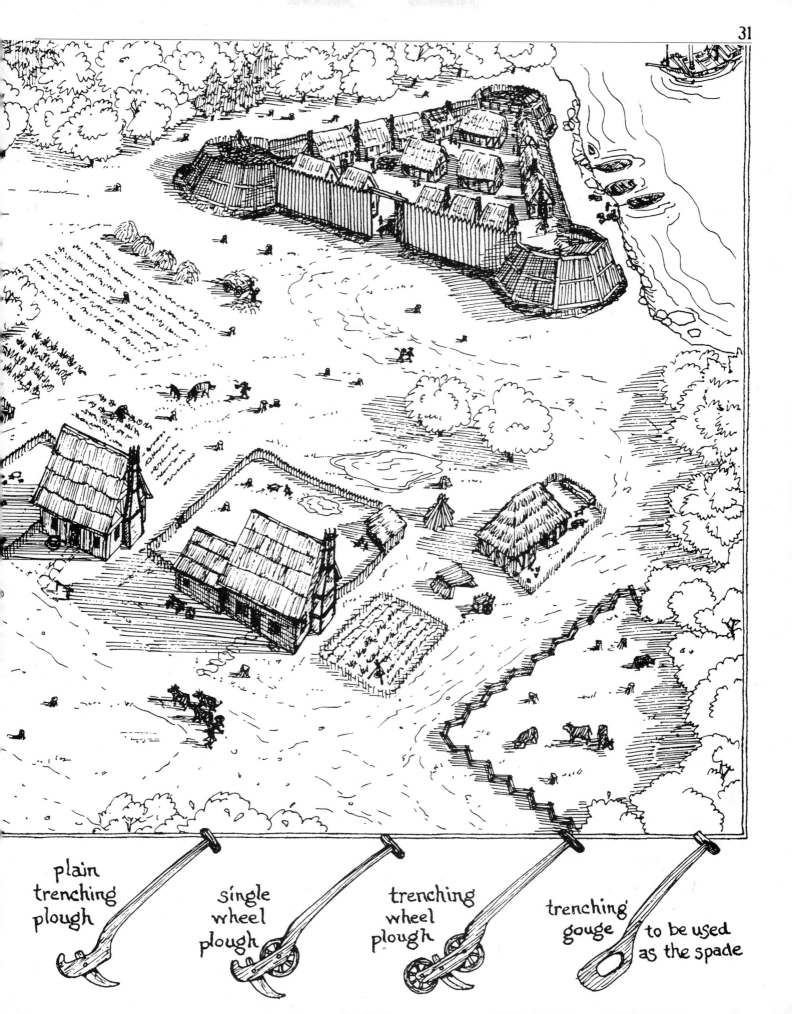

plain trenching plough

single wheel plough

trenching wheel plough

trenching gouge

to be used as the spade

Smoking Tobacco Is in Fashion

Most settlers were happy to make a home in Virginia. They had found a way to make money by growing tobacco.

Tobacco farmers, along with their boy servants, typically tended four acres and about 1,000 tobacco plants. They were able to produce about 250 pounds of tobacco on this amount of land. But if the hungry tobacco worms ate too much of the crop, this amount could be substantially less.

The tobacco was shipped in barrels to an ever-increasing smoking public in England. The high demand for tobacco caused its price to soar in the 1620s. The colonists made huge profits. They used tobacco like money. It was common for a planter to pay his debts with tobacco.

Tobacco, however, hadn't always been used for pleasure. Tobacco was first used as medicine. But that changed in the 1600s. Europeans found it enjoyable to smoke tobacco while having a drink with friends. Tobacco smokers were everywhere.

WHAT RIGHT?

In 1609 Robert Gray asked, "By what right . . . can we enter into the land of these savages [Indians], take away their rightfull inheritance from them, and plant ourselves in their places?"

Many Englishmen felt settlers didn't intend to take Indian land, but to share it. Besides, there was so much land, and such an abundance of resources and food. Surely, they believed, there was enough for everyone.

The settlers also believed that their English culture was superior to the culture of the "savages." They felt that they were helping the Indians by exposing them to their supposedly superior culture. It did not matter to them whether or not the Indians agreed with this self-centered opinion.

On March 22, 1622, Chief Opechancanough attacked Jamestown, killing 347 people.

The Powhatan Indians had had enough. They were tired of the English bullying them into providing corn because settlers couldn't grow enough. They were irritated by the English scorching their fields, out of sheer spitefulness, and attacking their people. They were alarmed by the ever-increasing white population.

Chief Opechancanough believed he had no other choice but to rid his people of the English. But his efforts proved hopeless. After the attack, most settlers didn't bother to restrain themselves from killing or enslaving Indians. From 1622 to 1632, the English and the Powhatan waged war.

SERVING THE NEEDY

Today local and federal governments provide services that attempt to help the poor and homeless. But in the 1600s the English poor and homeless had no services to assist them. All they had was the "poor law." This law gave the church the power to tax citizens so that it could provide help for the needy.

Poor and homeless families were most vulnerable to disease. A common cold could be deadly to someone living on the streets. Healthy adults and children had to be on their guard to avoid being arrested for begging. It was not uncommon for children as young as seven to be brought before the court as dangerous beggars.

No wonder many children were willing to leave their lives on the streets to become servants in Virginia. It had to be better than it was in England, they thought. But was it? A child servant served his Virginia master until he was twenty-one years old—unless the master gambled the child away in a game of chance. Planters often wagered their servants. Indentured servants were considered property, not people.

Child servants in Virginia had no choice but to accept their fate. There were few laws to protect them against cruel masters. Even if a brave servant managed to convince authorities to arrest his brutal master, the child would not be free—he or she would be forced to serve a new master.

WOMEN COME TO JAMESTOWN

On October 1, 1609, two women arrived at James Fort. Soon after, the first marriage in Virginia was celebrated. Such a celebration was rare. Few women dared to travel to Virginia, not after hearing stories of starvation and Indian attacks. Even the London Company doubted the colony's survival.

Ten years later, in 1619, all doubt had faded. The colonists were working hard to ensure the colony's prosperity. The London Company announced the departure of eleven ships with 1,261 passengers bound for Virginia. On these ships the company sent over ninety women to become the wives of the male settlers. Now it was time to encourage adventurous women to join adventurous men and help Virginia grow.

Two women arrived at James Fort.

Taken Away

The doctor pulled his lips apart to check his teeth.

The African boy stood gazing at the ocean for the very first time. He was fascinated by the ceaseless crashing of waves on the shore.

Suddenly a scream pierced the air. The boy remembered why he was standing on the beach. King Accra's warriors had attacked his village. They had killed his parents and any others who resisted. Everyone else had been captured. They had been led to a prison by the sea to await the arrival of an English slave ship.

Now the ship was here. All the prisoners waited their turn to be inspected by the English doctor on the beach. Those who passed inspection became English slaves. Those who were too old or who were injured could look forward to being the slaves of King Accra—or possibly to death.

The boy was next. The doctor squeezed his limbs and pulled his lips apart to check his teeth. He examined his eyes. The doctor was satisfied. He pushed the boy to one side. Two guards held him down, while a third pushed a hot iron into the boy's skin, branding his body with the company's mark. The boy screamed. He was now the property of an English company.

Wiping the tears from his eyes, he and the other approved slaves were returned to the prison. The English captain had hoped to leave with his human cargo the next day, but rough seas made boarding impossible.

This pleased the mighty African king of the Gold Coast. With the extra time, he hoped to press the English traders for more kettles, carpets, and guns in exchange for the slaves.

Five days later, when the sea calmed, the slaves were loaded into longboats. The

Slaves in Virginia

Growing crops in Virginia was miserable work. The days were hot, and mosquitoes constantly attacked the fieldworkers. With such harsh conditions, it was difficult to convince a settler to work someone else's land.

Bringing in slaves assured Virginia landowners of a labor supply. By the eighteenth century, the English were using more than 1,000 ships to bring 5,000 to 15,000 slaves a year from Africa to Virginia and the other English colonies.

boats were rowed out into the open sea toward the English ship anchored offshore.

The boy, who had loved looking at the ocean, was afraid to find himself surrounded by so much water. This would be his first ocean voyage. He was not alone. Like the boy, many of the prisoners had been taken from villages far inland, away from the ocean.

Many of the people couldn't bear the idea of leaving their homeland. The boy watched as men and women dove from the canoes into the ocean, holding themselves beneath the waves to avoid being recaptured. Few could swim. They preferred to drown off an African shore than to sail to a foreign land.

When the canoes reached the ship, the boy was hoisted aboard and immediately chained to another man. The boy and his mate were shoved down a hatch below deck. Others followed until the space was packed with people. The more slaves the captain delivered, the more he would be paid for his cargo.

The boy sat in the darkness, trying to ignore his upset stomach. He tried to stretch his legs. There was no room.

So the boy wondered. He wondered where he was going and if the new land would be like his home. He wondered what awaited him. He had plenty of time to wonder, to cry, and to dream of his homeland, gone now forever.

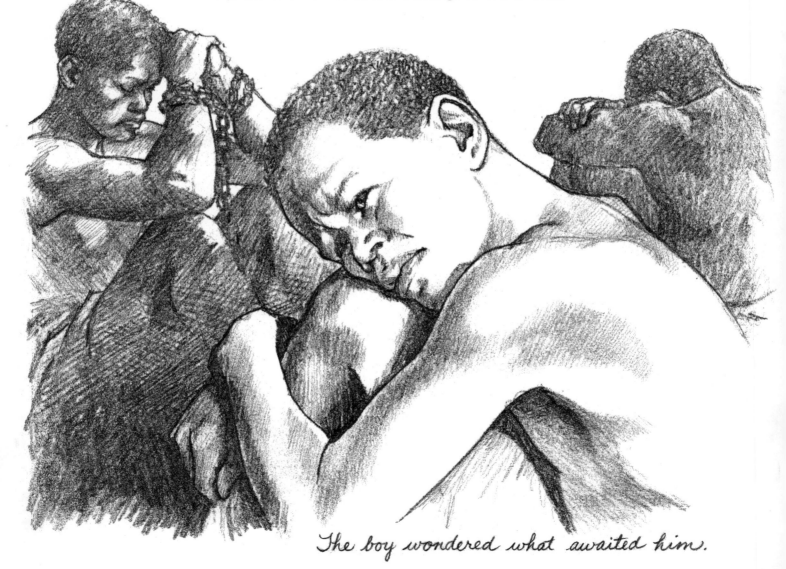

The boy wondered what awaited him.

THE INVISIBLE ENEMY

The shaman of the Indian village was deeply troubled. It was his responsibility to care for the health of his people.

Bird Nose, a young girl, saw that the shaman was upset. She could see that his mind wandered as they picked herbs for a health-renewing drink the villagers drank every spring.

"What is wrong?" asked the girl.

The shaman guided her to a tree and sat with her beneath its green web of leaves. He looked into the rising sun and said, "It was in this direction that the mighty Great Hare once created men and women. For a while, he held them in a great bag. . . ."

"Yes, I remember," stated the girl, unable to stop herself from interrupting the shaman. "The Hare did this to protect men and women from the other gods, the Four Winds. These four gods wanted to eat the men and women."

"It is foolish," admitted the shaman, "but I sometimes pray to the Great Hare to take our people and place them back in the bag. They need protection."

"Why?"

"Something is wrong. Too many people are dying."

Bird Nose was overcome with sorrow. She thought about her sister who had died last week, and her father who had died several months ago. Half of the villagers had perished in the last year.

"Perhaps the deer can help us," suggested the girl. "The Great Hare once released the men and women from the bag among vast herds of deer. And they were safe."

"I do not know," replied the shaman, standing up. "Let us finish our work."

The shaman and the girl returned to the village with their baskets of herbs. A white man rushed up to them. He had lived happily for many months in the village. But there was no happiness in him now. He was frightened.

"My wife is worse, much worse. Please come," he pleaded.

The shaman went to his house. Bird Nose followed. So did many of the villagers. He placed his basket of herbs down and gathered his healing tools.

When he entered the house of the sick Indian woman, she was lying on a mat. He knelt beside her. Her sickness was like so many others. It was "the pest."

"My wife is much worse. Please come."

Now the shaman's mind did not wander. He focused deeply on his work. He splashed water on himself, then he gathered up a rattle. He shook the rattle and beat his other hand against his chest. The shaman concentrated on this healing rhythm.

The shaman rose, very slowly, and circled the woman. He shook the rattle over her entire body very softly. He sprinkled water on her and then chanted. When he was done, he left and sprinkled herb-scented water around the house.

The husband thanked the shaman. The villagers returned to their work. The shaman went back to his house with the girl.

The shaman didn't speak. He sat in a corner with his head bowed. He knew that by morning the woman would be dead.

The shaman had the ability to communicate with the spiritual world. Spirits entered his body and gave him the power to heal. Where was his power now? The shaman could not stop "the pest." He could not heal his people.

English Diseases

In Europe the plague and smallpox were killing thousands of people. These deadly diseases traveled with the colonists to the New World. The colonists unknowingly passed these diseases on to the Indians they met. Soon the Indians were caught up in the same chain of disease and death.

But matters were far worse for the Indians. The English also brought over the cold and the flu. To the English these illnesses weren't usually life-threatening. They had grown up with them. But the Indians hadn't. What caused sickness in the colonists could bring death to the Indians.

At Home Among Whites

Francis leaned forward and fell down the riverbank.

The Pilgrims Come
to North America

English citizens had to belong to the Church of England, which was headed by the king. It was the law. Anyone who refused to join this church was in danger of being arrested.

In eastern England, some citizens separated from the Church of England to form their own congregation. They moved to the Netherlands to avoid persecution, but found they missed the English culture.

These people named themselves Pilgrims, mean-

"I'm going to catch eels," announced Squanto. The Patuxet Indian left the Pilgrims' settlement and headed for the river.

Francis Billington, a fourteen-year-old boy, secretly followed Squanto. When Squanto reached the river, Francis watched the Indian walk into the cold river that stood at low tide.

Squanto pushed his feet into the mud, and between his feet appeared a large eel. Squanto pulled the eel out with his hands.

Francis leaned forward to get a better look and fell down the pitched riverbank. He landed right beside Squanto. Francis stood up. An eel surfaced between Francis's feet.

"Quick, grab him," said Squanto.

Francis swallowed his fear, locked his hands around the eel's slimy body, and yanked it out of the mud. This was fun.

When they had caught enough eels, Francis and Squanto sat down to rest.

"How did you learn to catch eels?" asked Francis.

"I learned from my father and other men in my village."

"Where is your village?"

"It is gone, and so are all my people," replied Squanto. "Sickness killed them all."

"Why weren't you killed?" asked Francis.

"I wasn't here. I was kidnapped by Captain Hunt, who sold me into slavery in Spain. Thank God the priests there took pity on me. Later, I traveled back to England and then here. And now, before the sun sets, we should go back to your home."

"It can be your home, too," said Francis.

"I would like that," replied Squanto.

Francis and Squanto returned to the settlement, carrying a booty of fat eels. Everyone wanted to know how it was done. Squanto showed the Pilgrims how to catch eels and to net fish. He taught them how to grow healthy corn by using fish as fertilizer. He even helped organize a peace treaty between the neighboring Wampanoag and the Pilgrims.

Squanto's knowledge allowed the Pilgrim settlement to thrive. And in return Squanto was able to live among whites. It was here he felt at home.

THE MAYFLOWER COMPACT

Before the Pilgrims left the *Mayflower* to establish the Plymouth Colony, forty-one of the Pilgrims signed a document called the Mayflower Compact. This agreement, 187 words long, contained very unique principles.

The Pilgrims lived in a world in which the wealthy ruled the people. The Mayflower Compact was an agreement to establish a community in which all people were equal and the government was represented not by just the wealthy, but by everyone. The compact stated the Pilgrims' plan "to combine ourselves together into a civic body politic . . . to enact . . . just and equal laws."

The Pilgrims' beliefs weren't forgotten. They were the foundation upon which our nation, the United States of America, was established.

A MODEL PEACE TREATY

The peace treaty that Squanto helped negotiate between the Pilgrims and the Wampanoag was a remarkable agreement. The treaty spoke of respect, honesty, and friendship. The following are some of the treaty's agreements.

They agreed that no Wampanoag should injure any Pilgrim. If any Wampanoag did hurt any Pilgrim, the Wampanoag should send the person who committed the crime to the Pilgrims to be punished.

The Wampanoag and the Pilgrims also agreed that when they met, they should leave their weapons behind. And if there was ever an unjust war carried out against the Pilgrims or the Wampanoag they should come to each other's aid.

REMEMBERING TO GIVE THANKS

The Pilgrims were thankful to be alive and thankful to the Wampanoag for their guidance and gifts of corn.

William Bradford, governor of the colony, remembered celebrating Thanksgiving Day in Leyden, Holland, where he lived and practiced his faith without harassment. This celebration marked the anniversary of the city's rescue from Spanish occupiers. He decided the colony would have its own Thanksgiving Day.

Massasoit, the Indian chief, was sent an invitation. The Indians were familiar with a holiday of giving thanks. They had a yearly celebration, in the fall, to give thanks for the corn harvest.

The Pilgrims' first Thanksgiving Day, in 1621, was a feast of food and entertainment.

The Indians and the Pilgrims both provided food. The meal was an assortment of vegetables, meats, and dried wild fruits. There were even individual pies that were made by placing fruit inside small dough casings.

For entertainment, there were shooting and bow-and-arrow competitions, as well as footraces and wrestling. Miles Standish, the leader of the colony's defense, showed his men's skill by presenting a series of marching maneuvers.

It was a day of joy and peace, a day to give thanks. It is this spirit that we continue to honor every year when we celebrate Thanksgiving Day.

ing homeless travelers. On September 16, 1620, more than one hundred Pilgrims left the Netherlands to sail to the English colony in North America. It was a rough journey. Their ship, the Mayflower, *was blown off course. Instead of arriving off the coast of Virginia, the Pilgrims arrived hundreds of miles to the north, off the coast of what is now Massachusetts. The Pilgrims called their colony Plymouth.*

The Pilgrims had few resources. Their neighbors, the Wampanoag (wom-peh-NOH-ag) Indians, helped the Pilgrims even though the Pilgrims were stealing their corn. The Wampanoag did this in hopes of finding an ally to help them fight their enemies, the Narragansett (nar-eh-GAN-set).

Between Two Worlds

He had to repeat the essay to his tutor.

Indian Giver

"Indian giver" is an insult still used today. It stands for a person who gives something to someone else and then takes it back.

This insult is based on a misunderstanding between the English settlers and the Indians.

Indians didn't believe land could be owned. The English did. When the English traded for land, the English felt they owned the land. The Indians felt the English could work the land.

If the English, for some reason, didn't work the land, then the Indians felt there was no reason why they shouldn't use it themselves. This angered the English. The Indians gave them land, then took it away.

Had the English taken the time to understand the Indian idea of "owning" land, the insult "Indian giver" might never have been invented.

It was Saturday. John Sassamon, a Wampanoag Indian, sat memorizing an essay on religious teachings. He had to repeat the essay, word for word, to his tutor, John Eliot, a Puritan who had converted Sassamon and other Indians to the Puritan faith.

Sassamon was used to studying, just as he was used to his English name and his English-style clothing. He was very friendly with whites. He had even fought alongside them when they attacked Indian villages.

Now he was learning to be a minister. Sassamon hoped to preach in the town of Natick. He knew the English Bible well.

When Sassamon finally traveled to Natick to preach, he prayed his congregation would see him not as an Indian, but simply as a minister. They didn't. He was an oddity, worthy of distrust, not acceptance.

Sassamon eventually left white society to live among the Wampanoag, near the Plymouth Colony. He became an assistant to Metacom, the supreme chief of the Wampanoag. Metacom was known to the whites as "King Phillip."

Metacom despised the whites. Their desire to convert his people to the Puritan faith threatened his tribe's unity.

Metacom refused to live under white rule or to move away. He decided to attack the Plymouth and Boston settlements. With Sassamon's knowledge of whites, Metacom hoped to improve his chances of winning.

Sassamon found himself in a dilemma. Discovering Metacom's plan, he was faced with the painful question: To whom am I loyal? Sassamon could either stand by Metacom or inform the white leaders of the attack.

Sassamon warned the leaders of the Plymouth Colony. Soon after, he was killed by three Indians. Plymouth officials found an Indian who said he saw the men who murdered Sassamon. Three Wampanoag men were arrested and brought to trial. They were convicted and executed.

To the Pilgrims and the Puritans, the trial was proof that Metacom was behind Sassamon's killing. Retaliation was the only way to respond to Metacom's willful ways. In 1675 the Metacom War began.

PURITANS CRITICIZE THE CHURCH

The Puritans, like the Pilgrims, didn't want to belong to the Church of England. The Puritans disagreed with the church's beliefs. They maintained that the king should make the church's ceremonies less complicated.

The king wouldn't stand for such criticism. He ordered the Puritans to be arrested and jailed.

In 1630 the Puritans left England and traveled to Massachusetts. They settled at the mouth of the Charles River, to the north of the Pilgrim settlement. The Puritans called their settlement Boston and their colony the Massachusetts Bay Colony.

The Puritans were more fortunate than the Pilgrims. They were a wealthier people. They sailed with fifteen ships filled with tools and supplies.

These resources helped make it easier to establish their settlement and to get on with their mission to convert Indians to the Puritan faith.

A PEACE TREATY OF YOUR OWN

When nations settle a dispute, such as a war, they sign a peace treaty. This document states the agreement that has resolved the nations' shared problems.

When friends settle a dispute it is rarely concluded with the creation and signing of a peace treaty. But it can be.

The next time you have a falling out with a friend, a parent, or a sibling, don't just end the dispute with a handshake or a hug. Sit down with the person and create a peace treaty that will hopefully secure the continuation of your friendship.

This treaty must contain statements both people agree on. There can be a statement about the settlement, which includes a brief summary of the argument and how the problem has been resolved. There can be a statement of conduct, which addresses how each person agrees to treat the other person. Finally, there can be a statement about your relationship, which mentions the reasons why you are friends.

This treaty can be an important document, if you want it to be. Take the time to personalize your treaty. Create other statements that include activities you do together or ideas you both share.

By working together to write this peace treaty, you and your friend will have a deeper understanding of your friendship's importance.

It Started with Henry

The Indians were invited to board the ship.

Henry Hudson dreamed of finding a passage through the Arctic Ocean that would take him around the North Pole and down into India. He outfitted a ship and explored the frozen region until problems forced him back. Most of the Arctic was unknown, and the maps that he used were sometimes based upon guesswork.

But Hudson refused to give up. After his second voyage, his exploits brought him respect and fame. The Dutch, who were leaders in world trade, believed he was close to finding that passage through the Arctic. A Dutch business called the East India Company hired him to go exploring, but under two conditions. Hudson must only go north, and if he ran into trouble, he must come straight back to Holland. If he didn't return, the company would pay his wife, Katharine, a widow's settlement of 200 guilders.

Hudson agreed. In 1609 he left on the sturdy *Halve Maen* (*Half Moon*). His crew of Dutch and English sailors included Robert Juet, an Englishman who kept a diary during the voyage. As the *Halve Maen* sailed north beyond Norway, the weather grew colder. The sails froze, and blocks of ice caked the ropes. The sailors refused to sail in the treacherous waters. They mutinied.

Hudson couldn't control his crew. Breaking his agreement with the Dutch company, he turned south. No one knew that he had brought with him a map and some letters written by Captain John Smith of the Virginia Colony. If the map was right, Hudson believed that he could sail up the rivers of North America and reach India from the west.

In the summer of 1609, Hudson and his crew spotted a great body of water in the distance. They sailed into what is now called Upper Bay, New York, and anchored off a small island. Some Indians approached. Juet's diary said they wore copper ornaments. The Indians were invited to board the ship. Soon they were trading their corn for European knives and beads.

As they continued their exploring, the ship entered a wide, deep river dotted with islands. Juet was moved to write poetry:

Then the sun arose,
And we steered away north again,
And saw the land from the west
By north to the north-west by north,
All like broken islands.

They called this the Great River, or just the River. Juet described an island he called Mannahata, perhaps a change in the word *Mahican*, meaning "wolf," for the tribe of Indians who lived there. Once Hudson went to an Indian supper in an oak bark house, where he sat on a floor mat and ate roast pigeon and dog.

In early October, Hudson prepared for the return voyage. Sailing downriver, the crew traded Indian furs for clothing and knives.

When Hudson finally reported to the Dutch, they were disappointed. His voyage, sailing up the Great River and trading for Indian furs, didn't interest them. They sent someone else to explore the Arctic.

English businessmen hired Hudson for his next, and last, voyage. He and his crew started out on a ship called the *Discovery*. They hadn't sailed very far before his sailors began fighting. They were jealous when Hudson gave out special favors. It was a poor way to begin a long sea voyage.

Hudson sailed toward Greenland, carrying translations of early Norse maps and papers. He saw glaciers that Eirik the Red had seen 600 years before. Sometimes the ship anchored beside ice floes and the men played on the ice. They saw polar bears.

But the farther they went, the worse things became. Fog and ice surrounded them. Some of the crew believed they were lost. But this time Hudson refused to turn back. When it grew so cold they were forced to stop for the winter, they anchored at a place now called Hudson Bay. Within days, the *Discovery* was frozen in the ice.

While they were trapped during that winter of 1611, their plight grew worse. Scurvy attacked them. Hudson tried to ration the last food, which led to fighting. He accused some men of stealing. Many sailors became his enemies.

One night three of them caught him off guard. They tied him up and seized the ship. Hudson was forced into a small boat, along with his son and seven others. They were set adrift. Henry Hudson and the unfortunate sailors were never seen again.

GETTING TO KNOW YOU

The East India Company didn't care that Hudson traded with Indians for beaver skins. But traders in Amsterdam knew Germans and Russians who would pay a fortune for warm skins. They returned to explore the Great River. They hoped to get otter and beaver skins without trespassing in New France (now called Canada).

In 1614 Dutch traders claimed the land between New France and Virginia and called it New Netherland. After they set up trading posts along the river, they needed farming families to grow food for the fur traders.

The Dutch West India Company was formed. In 1623 it hired thirty Dutch families to settle in New Netherland for one year. Among the first colonists were Johannes de Laet, who recorded the company's history, and Kiliaen van Rensselaer, an Amsterdam jeweler.

At first the colonists split up, but within two years they gathered together on one island, which they named New Amsterdam. Today it is known as Manhattan. The Mahican Indians welcomed the Dutch (it is said that they were surprised by their wooden shoes) and made friendship pacts with them. The colonist Caterina Trico reported that the Mahican were "all as quiet as Lambs."

Soon a brisk business was underway, with Indians trading their prized furs for kettles, knives, beads, and thick woolen cloth. A few months later, a Dutch colonist wrote home to say that the settlers lived "in friendship with the natives."

Those Flag-Waving Crabs

Henry Hudson claimed the land between New France (Canada) and Virginia for the Dutch. His mistake was that he didn't mark its boundaries. Before long, the English colonists were plotting ways to claim the rich Manhattan farmland and the Hudson River for themselves. But David de Vries, a Dutch colonist, believed Mother Nature had decided who should own the country.

Just look at the crabs of New Netherland, de Vries said. They show that the Dutch ought to populate this land. The crabs' claws "are the colour of the flag of our Prince: orange, white, and blue."

They were set adrift.

WE'LL TAKE MANHATTAN

In countries where winter meant blizzards and deep snow, a warm beaver-skin coat was a luxurious possession and a sign of wealth. When the fur wore off the skin, the hide made a great hat. People found other uses for beaver, too. One scientist believed the beaver's flat tail was actually a fish!

Some people lined their fireplace mantels with beaver skins. Others believed that beaver slippers not only kept your feet warm but also cured an ailment known as gout.

Folk medicine called for a dash of beaver oil to treat poor eyesight, dizziness, stomach pains, toothaches, and "lameness." Beaver testicles, called "cods," were reported to bring sleep when smelled. Taken with a glass of water, they were thought to "remove idiocy."

On May 4, 1626, Peter Minuit arrived in New Netherland on the ship *Meeuwken* (*Seagull*). Proud to be the new director of New Netherland, he came to take care of some legal business with the Indians. He knew the English and French were not pleased to see the Dutch settling the lands between them. For their protection, Minuit brought the Dutch colonists together in one location. In addition, he hoped to do something no other colonists in North America had done before.

Peter Minuit hoped to *buy* Manhattan Island from the Indians. An island would be an easy place to defend, and this one, 14,000 acres, had fine harbors for ship traffic, forested hills for building homes, and rich soil for farming. If the Dutch owned it, would the French or English dare start trouble? Minuit called the Canarsie Indian chief to a council to discuss the sale.

The price of Manhattan Island today, with all its buildings, would probably run somewhat over $40 billion. Peter Minuit got the land for sixty Dutch guilders worth of hatchets, clothing, and other goods. His price was estimated to equal about $24, but experts now figure it was closer to $2,000.

Minuit probably deserves credit for wanting to buy Manhattan Island. Other colonists used force to take Indian lands when they wanted them. But there were some problems with this sale. First, the Indians who lived there thought of the land as Mother Earth, not as a piece of real estate that could be traded away or sold. The Dutch had a different idea about property, and we don't know that the chief understood what the "sale" meant to the Dutch. Second, more than one tribe lived on the island. To be fair, any decision about it should have included the Algonquin leaders and others whose people used the land.

Peter Minuit was probably happy with the deal he made. The Dutch began building a fort on Manhattan and started a town they named New Amsterdam. But buying Manhattan did not solve problems the way the Dutch hoped it would.

Peter Minuit hoped to buy Manhattan Island from the Indians.

They dug their first houses out of the earth.

A Quick Dutch Lesson

When the Dutch settled on Manhattan, they kept the basic name the Indians called it, but gave it a more "Dutch-like" sound. They did this with other places, too, changing Indian names a bit or choosing entirely new Dutch names.

When the English took over New Amsterdam, they fiddled with Dutch spellings, to make them look more English. If you look at the old Dutch names, you may see a pattern—especially with vowels. How good a word detective are you? Can you match these lists of old Dutch and "new" York places?

Hopoakan	Schenectady
Haerlem	Yonkers
Jonkheers	Great
Scheaen-	Brooklyn
hechstede	Hoboken
Bronck	Harlem
Breukelyn	Bronx
Groote	

NEW HOMES IN NEW AMSTERDAM

The first job of the adults who came to New Netherland was to build homes for their families. In the beginning, they cared only about making warm, safe shelters. They dug their first houses out of the earth. Bark lined the inside walls. Sod, which is large chunks of grass and roots, covered the roof. Sometimes, instead of a dugout house, they built a frame of saplings, or young tree trunks, and filled in the cracks with bark and sod.

When their farmland was cleared and young crops were sprouting, there was more time to think of building large, solid, permanent homes. These were often made of stone, very much like their old homes in the Netherlands. Some of the details that made Dutch architecture distinctive are still copied in homes today.

You might have seen traditional Dutch architecture without realizing it. The first thing you notice is the unusual shape of the roof. Instead of dropping down in one long slope from the point at the top, the Dutch roof, called a gambrel roof, slopes, or "pitches," twice, creating more space in the attic. It's used on barns as well as houses.

Another popular characteristic of Dutch homes that is copied everywhere is the front porch at the top of a few steps. Holland is a country that lies below sea level. To avoid the problem of wet feet and floors, it made good sense to raise the front door. To enter the house, the Dutch built steps up to a *stoep*, a platform or landing, usually with a railing around it, above the street. The colonists in New Netherland were glad to find that the streets didn't flood the way they did at home. Even so, they liked their front *stoep* and wouldn't give it up! We call it a porch.

Another practical creation of the Dutch is the split front door, with a top half that could be opened for light or fresh air while the lower section stayed latched, or locked. On elaborate homes, thick panes or panels of glass, sometimes made from bottles, also let light in the top.

More people soon moved into the Province of New Netherland, settling throughout the Hudson Valley, the islands in the bays, and the Dutch communities of New Jersey. Many liked the solid Dutch architecture and copied it for their own homes. On your next trip through the neighborhoods of your community or to the city, look at the houses you pass. See if you can spot roofs, porches, or double doors that show the influence of early Dutch builders in America.

TROUBLE IN PARADISE

The Dutch developed good farms and a profitable fur trade. They tolerated people with other beliefs, partly because they believed hardworking residents strengthened the colony. Puritans and Jews, who were persecuted in the English colonies, moved north to New Netherland.

The English envied Dutch progress. It was said that the Dutch owned more ships than houses. They ruled the fishing industry in Europe. Queen Elizabeth I ordered the English to eat fish three times a week, but it didn't improve the English fishing trade. After her death, her nephew King James I tried to tax Dutch fisheries. The Dutch refused to pay.

The English also resented the Dutch whaling trade and the spice trade. With the Dutch claiming land in America, where would it end? King James wasn't sure, but the years of tolerance were about to end.

In 1652 the Dutch asked England to help mark a permanent boundary between their colonies. The English replied that they didn't know of *any* Dutch territory, except some plantations along the Hudson River (a name the Dutch did not recognize). A month later, a Dutch ship sailed in the English Channel and wouldn't lower its flag in respect to the British. A sea battle broke out that became a two-year war.

The Anglo-Dutch war in Europe did not spill over into the colonies, but the Dutch strengthened Fort Amsterdam and built a 2,340-foot wall around the edge of town. The path beside it, possibly the most famous street in the world, was called Wall Street.

In 1659 the English government decided to send settlers up the "Hudson River" to open a trading post. "What Hudson River?" the Dutch asked. It was the North River to them, and they didn't want any more settlers who were loyal to the English king to move in. But they weren't equipped to start trouble with the English.

When King Charles I took the English throne in 1660, he had a surprise for the Province of New Netherland. He claimed it for England, and promptly *gave* it to his brother James, the Duke of York.

The Dutch governor of New Netherland, Peter Stuyvesant, a man with a peg leg, was trying to keep peace with everyone so Dutch trade could continue. He was slow to realize that the English wanted to destroy the Dutch hold on world shipping and products.

On August 26, 1664, Stuyvesant was shocked when he heard that King Charles had given New Amsterdam to his brother. But King Charles added that the Dutch could keep their land and businesses. He said that very little would change. But Stuyvesant refused to surrender New Amsterdam. Even four enemy warships and 2,000 British soldiers couldn't persuade him. Finally, his close friends made the decision for him. They didn't want bloodshed.

They gave Stuyvesant a petition signed by ninety-three important citizens. Even his son had signed it. The Dutch accepted English rule. The port city was renamed New York, in honor of the duke who took it. The next day, the English flag flew over the fort on Manhattan.

Fingers in the *Koekje* Jar

Whenever a new nationality comes to America, they bring along their favorite recipes. Gradually these foods spread among new friends in the neighborhood. Favorite foods among the Dutch were oysters and cabbage—which they chopped into *koolslaa* (coleslaw) or brined as sauerkraut. Those might not be your favorites, but would you turn down waffles or chocolate-chip cookies? For holidays like Christmas, the Dutch pressed wooden cookie molds over sweet anise-seed dough to make special shapes. While you thank the Dutch for bringing *koekjes* to America, try this version of an old Dutch favorite at home. Anise seed gives the cookies a licorice flavor.

Anise Sugar Koekjes
(Makes two dozen cookies)
2 cups sifted white flour
1 tsp. baking powder
¼ tsp. salt
½ cup margarine, softened
¾ cup sugar
1 egg
¼ cup milk
1½ tsp. vanilla extract
1 Tbsp. anise seed
½ cup raw or white sugar, for dipping

Preheat oven to 350 degrees, and grease two cookie sheets.
1. In a large bowl, sift together flour, baking powder, and salt.
2. In a separate bowl, cream together margarine and sugar. When smooth, add the egg and beat well.
3. Stir the dry ingredients into the sugar mixture, and slowly add the milk, vanilla, and anise seed. Dough will be slightly sticky.
4. Spoon dough by heaping teaspoons onto cookie sheet, leaving 2 inches between cookies. (Each cookie sheet will hold twelve cookies.)
5. Use the bottom of a glass or mug to flatten cookies by first dipping the bottom into water so sugar sticks and then into a bowl filled with ½ cup sugar. Continue dipping glass into sugar and flattening cookies.
6. Bake cookies at 350 degrees for 9 to 12 minutes, or until lightly browned around edges. With hot pads, remove cookie sheets from oven, and use a spatula to transfer cookies to platter to cool.

The Courage of Patience

Patience Scott was born in 1648 to Katherine and Richard Scott. The Scott family followed the Quakers' beliefs, such as equality for all people and refusing to physically harm another person. The following story is based on an actual event.

Her mother was whipped in public.

Several Quaker men had arrived with bad news from Boston. Patience Scott rushed to Mary Dyer's house. Patience's mother, Katherine, was close behind. As they entered the house, Patience saw the men were upset and exhausted. It was forty hard miles from Boston, Massachusetts, to Mary Dyer's home in Providence, Rhode Island.

"It is getting worse," sighed one man. "The Puritans are torturing Quakers now, as well as imprisoning them. I have seen Quaker men walk the streets with one ear cut off, or the letters S L branded on their cheek."

Patience was horrified. "What do these letters mean?" she asked.

"They stand for 'seditious libeler' [treasonous liar].'"

"This is not all," said the other man. "Puritan officials search Quakers as they arrive by ship. They take off people's clothing, looking for markings of a witch. They search their belongings and burn their books. Some Quakers are being shipped as slaves to the island of Barbados. Something must be done."

That night, Patience couldn't sleep. She kept hearing the man's plea that "something must be done." She knew her mother and Mary desperately wanted to help, but they could not. Patience remembered her first visit to Boston with her mother and Mary. She would never forget helplessly watching as her mother was whipped in public for protesting against Quaker persecution. Nor was it possible to forget the threat of being hanged if they returned.

Patience grew angry. "The man is right," she thought. "Something must be done. I wonder why I can't go to Boston? They surely wouldn't hang an eleven-year-old girl!"

Mind Your Thees and Thous, and That Hat

Under Puritan law, it was respectful to use the word *you* when speaking to another person. When a Quaker addressed someone, he used *thou*, or *thee*. Puritans regarded these words as rude.

Quakers didn't use these words to be rude. They simply thought that using the word *you* when speaking with people was confusing. Here's an example to demonstrate the Quakers' point.

When a person says, "Hey, you," it is impossible to tell if the person is calling out to one person or to two people. By using *thee* when speaking with one person, and *thou* when speaking with more than one person, it is easier to understand who the speaker is talking to.

Now what about the hat? Under Puritan law, it was common practice to tip your hat to an official or a minister. It was a sign of respect.

Quakers refused to tip their hats. They believed everyone was equal; therefore, it was unnecessary for people to tip their hats to anyone.

Patience made up her mind. The next day she convinced some Quaker missionaries to join her. That evening, Patience secretly left her house. Patience arrived in Boston one evening at dusk, after days of traveling. One of the missionaries guided them to a safe haven.

"Watch your step," the man cautioned.

He took them down Scott's Alley beneath a house. The air smelled of foul water and wood from the nearby marsh and saw pit. As they were about to leave the alley, two dock officials walked by. They hid in the shadows and waited.

"This way," the man whispered.

They turned right onto North Street.

"Here it is."

They went inside the Red Lyon Inn. It was empty. Tables and chairs were tossed about. The floor was littered with broken glass. Nicholas Upshall, the innkeeper, stopped cleaning.

"Sir, what took place here?" asked Patience.

"Don't worry, it happens all too often. It's my punishment for defending Quakers."

"Is it safe to stay here?" Patience cautiously asked.

"As safe as it is anywhere in Boston for Quakers," replied the innkeeper with a warm smile.

The next day, Patience stood before her companions and said, "I know what my mother would do if she were here. And I shall do no less. Follow me to the cathedral and let us protest the crimes against Quakers before the Puritan congregation and their minister."

It was a dangerous invitation. As the men decided what to do, Patience walked over to the innkeeper and asked for some empty bottles.

"Are you with me?" she asked the men.

"We are," they replied.

She handed each of them a bottle, which they hid beneath their clothing. They left the inn and headed toward the church.

Along the way, Puritans hurled insults at them. Patience said nothing, but the taunts confirmed her belief that protest was vital. When they reached the church, Patience was covered in goosebumps. It was from this same church that her mother had been dragged outside and whipped. For a moment, Patience hesitated to open the door. She wondered if she too would be whipped.

"Let's go," she said.

They entered the church and stood in the back. When the sermon was finished, Patience and her companions smashed their empty bottles on the floor. That was their protest. Just as the bottles were empty, so too was the Puritan faith empty of truth for supporting Quaker persecution.

The protesters were immediately surrounded and taken to jail. Patience was placed in a cell. For two months she was kept there without nourishing food, with no candle at night or visitors to speak with. On September 12, 1659, Patience was brought to trial. The court accused her of being an instrument of the devil. They declined to hang her because of her age. Instead, Patience Scott was released and ordered to return to her home in Rhode Island.

Not long after her return, Patience's elder sister, Mary Scott, heard her husband had been imprisoned in Boston along with seventeen other Quakers. Mary Scott had to go to Boston. Mary Dyer was eager to accompany her. She didn't care about the Puritan officials' threat to hang her. She had to help rescue her friend's husband and the other Quakers.

In early October 1659, they left for Boston. Within a week of their arrival, Mary Scott and Mary Dyer were arrested. Mary Dyer and several male companions were sentenced to be hanged. Mary Scott was whipped thirty times and ordered to leave Boston within five days.

On the day of Mary Dyer's execution, she watched her two male companions hanged upon the gallows. Mary was blindfolded and led up the ladder. The noose was placed around her neck.

Mary awaited her death. Reverend Wilson, who was in charge of executions, turned to the hangman. He ordered him to remove the noose from Mary's neck. He had no intention of hanging her, just scaring her. Mary Dyer was sent back to Rhode Island.

As horrifying as this experience was, Mary Dyer couldn't stay away. Carrying a roll of linen, she returned to Boston. Again, Mary was arrested. She knew this time she wouldn't escape the hangman's noose. That was why she brought the linen, so her dead body could be wrapped in the cloth.

Mary was led up the ladder and hanged until she was dead. She was wrapped in the linen she had brought from home and buried.

America's First Women's Club

Patience Scott's aunt, Anne Hutchinson, was also known for her protests against the intolerance of the Puritans. She is most remembered for her defiant statement that God talked directly to her. This declaration threatened the Puritan religious leaders, who believed it was their job to speak for God.

Anne Hutchinson is less well known for her support of women's rights. She was disturbed to see women doing housework without being able to enjoy any recreation. Unlike men, who spent their days outdoors, women needed a place to meet and talk for recreation. Anne Hutchinson offered her house, and by doing so she started America's first women's club.

PLAIN FRIENDS

Quakers are members of a religious group called the Society of Friends. The word *quaker* was used the first time in England, by someone who tried to make fun of them for "quaking in the sight of God." The Friends were not upset. They thought quaking, or shaking, made a good name. They decided to call themselves Quakers.

Time has brought changes to some of the practices of the Friends, but they still believe in simple living and equality for all. They still gather in plain meetinghouses instead of churches, usually without special church leaders or worship rituals. They worship in prayer, quietly awaiting the word of God, the "Inner Light," in their hearts. For centuries, Friends have followed what they believed were God's laws even if they are punished for breaking people's laws.

In England, Quakers did not remove their hats in the presence of the king. They refused to act as though he was better than ordinary people. For disobedience such as this, English Quakers were tortured, thrown into jail, or killed. They were also persecuted in the Massachusetts Colony by the Puritans. Many Quakers fled to Rhode Island, North Carolina, New Jersey, and Pennsylvania. There they had greater freedom to practice their religion without persecution.

Start

Finish

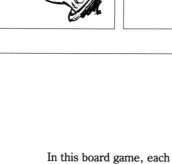
2

3

4

TO HIRE

22

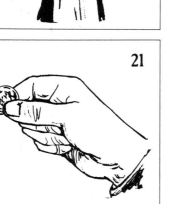
21

20

Road to

In this board game, each player represents a Quaker who lives in Boston and wants to move to Rhode Island. Just imagine you have no money to buy a cart to carry your belongings. To win you must earn a minimum of five coins and safely reach the finish. (Actually, in the colonies, people traded services or were paid in goods such as tobacco. Coins were in circulation but in such short supply that their use was impractical. However, for the sake of convenience, this game will use coins.)

You Will Need:

A die, some pennies, some tokens made out of cardboard, paper, and pencils.

Rules:

1. To determine who goes first, each player tosses the die. The player with the highest number goes first. (You can play by yourself, too.) Players must roll the die each time it is their turn.

2. If you land on a jail space, the only way to get out is to roll any odd number. If you roll a 3, then move ahead three spaces. If you roll an even number, you must wait until your next turn, then try again.

3. If you land on a square that asks you to give up a coin, but you have no coin, the game simply continues.

4. If you land on the Start/Finish square it means nothing, unless a player is starting or finishing.

5. Keep track of your earnings and losses on a piece of paper.

6. Once you have five coins you must continue playing until you reach Finish. You do not have to roll the exact number in order to reach Finish; you can roll a larger number than is needed.

Square 1 Start/Finish
Square 2 Earn one coin working at the mill.
Square 3 Watch a Quaker whipped in public. You say nothing.
Square 4 Hear of an opportunity to work. Move ahead three spaces.
Square 5 You are robbed. One coin taken.

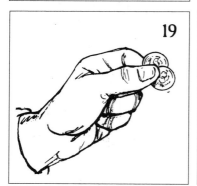
19

18

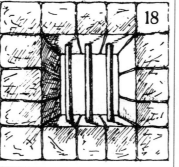
17

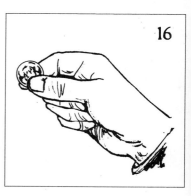
16

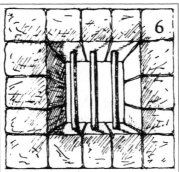

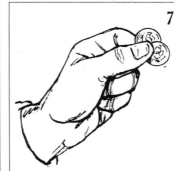

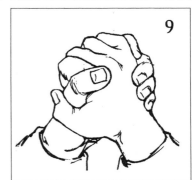

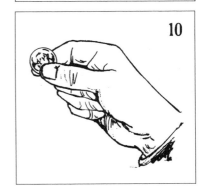

Freedom

Square 6 Jail. You are arrested for not going to church.

Square 7 Make a friend at Boston Wharf. Earn two coins by working on the dock.

Square 8 You need to recover from being whipped. Rest at Red Lyon Inn. Lose one turn.

Square 9 You need to pray. Move ahead four spaces to the meetinghouse.

Square 10 Earn one coin working for a shoemaker.

Square 11 Lose a coin. It falls out of a hole in your clothing!

Square 12 Jail. You are arrested for not tipping your hat to an official.

Square 13 The Quaker meetinghouse is raided. You must hide. Lose one turn.

Square 14 You become ill. You must spend one coin on treatment, if you have the money.

Square 15 A Puritan man hears of your woodworking skills and offers a job. Move ahead four spaces.

Square 16 You find a lost coin. Add one coin to your earnings.

Square 17 Go to the meetinghouse to take part in a discussion on Bible stories. Move back four spaces.

Square 18 Jail. You are arrested for using *thee* while speaking to a Puritan minister.

Square 19 Earn two coins making a hutch for a Puritan family.

Square 20 Enjoy a conversation with a fellow Quaker who has just come from Rhode Island.

Square 21 Earn one coin putting cobblestones down on North Street.

Square 22 A woman gives a fine sermon on the importance of nonviolence.

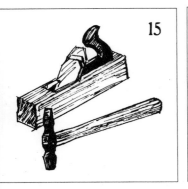

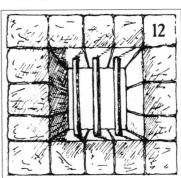

All Are Welcome

"Tell me about this bird, Aaron, this parrot," pleaded Matthew Collins.

"Their feathers are bright green," said Aaron, closing his eyes. "But when the parrots take flight, their wings reveal bright blue, yellow, and purple feathers. They are winged rainbows. But I love the monkeys best. They remind me of my little brother, so naughty they are."

"This past home of yours, Brazil, sounds so wild, so splendid. Did you have to leave?" Matthew asked.

"If we didn't, the Portuguese would have put us to death because we wouldn't renounce our Jewish faith and become Catholics," Aaron answered.

"We suffered similar hardships in Boston. Quakers were treated terribly. We, too, had to leave," Matthew replied.

Aaron and Matthew stopped talking. They looked down toward the water and watched the men making a boat. For a moment, they each thought about the suffering they had endured before coming to Newport, Rhode Island.

"Oh, my goodness!" exclaimed Matthew, standing up. "I forgot. I was supposed to go down to the wharf and claim a part of the cow. Come on."

Aaron and Matthew raced down Thames Street and turned onto the wharf. Aaron followed Matthew as he made his way through the crowd. In the center of the wharf stood a cow covered with chalk marks. Standing beside the cow was the butcher hold-

Aaron looked the cow over.

Roger Williams Founds a Colony

The Massachusetts Bay Colony expelled many people for not obeying Puritan laws. Roger Williams was one of them.

In 1636 Williams founded the Rhode Island Colony. It was the first colony to state in its rules that no person should be in "any wise molested, punished, disquieted, or called in question for any difference of opinion."

This rule was an amazing announcement. For the first time a colony was being founded on the principle that no person should be attacked for his or her beliefs.

This rule became known to people around the world who suffered religious persecution. From nearby, Massachusetts's Quakers moved to Rhode Island. And from even farther away, Jews from Brazil came to the new colony to be free.

Rhode Island was the real beginning of America's quest to be a nation of people who believe in freedom for all.

ing a chalk stick. Aaron looked the cow over, searching for unmarked portions. Fortunately, there were still some good sections available.

"Who is next?" asked the butcher.

Matthew spoke up, "The Collins family would like a shoulder and a midsection."

The butcher took his chalk and marked two sections of the cow. When it was completely marked, the butcher would slaughter the cow, and everyone would buy those portions they had reserved.

"Do you want to buy some meat?" Matthew asked Aaron.

"No, I don't think so," he replied.

"I never see you or any of the other Jews come down here to buy meat," stated Matthew as they walked back up the wharf.

"We can't buy the meat. It is not kosher."

"Ko-sher?" questioned Matthew with a puzzled look.

"In the Jewish faith no meat may be eaten unless it is slaughtered in a special way and blessed by a rabbi with special prayers."

"Do Jews think there is something evil about the cow on the wharf?" Matthew demanded.

"Matthew, please," said Aaron, noticing his friend's annoyed look. "No. Nothing is wrong with the cow. It just hasn't been sanctified. That is our way. It is not your way."

"Watch out," he shouted.

Matthew and Aaron walked up the wharf toward Aaron's house. Matthew waited for Aaron to start pressing him to become a Jew. Aaron waited for Matthew to start pressing him to become a Quaker. But neither boy tried to convince the other his religion was better. Instead, they returned to talking about Brazil, their favorite topic.

Matthew and Aaron passed the blacksmith. "Aaron," called the blacksmith.

"Yes, Mr. Johnson," replied Aaron.

"Come here, Aaron. I need your help."

Aaron and Matthew walked into the barn. Above the straw-covered floor was Aaron's family's enormous ox, nervously swaying in the air. It was hanging from a sturdy scaffold, strapped in by a wide leather band around its belly. This was the only way to put shoes on an ox. The ox was too heavy and its hooves were too small to stand on three hooves while the blacksmith shod one.

"This beast isn't behaving, Aaron," snapped the blacksmith. "Watch out," he shouted. The ox almost kicked Matthew in the chest. "Aaron, stand in front of the beast," ordered the blacksmith. "Not too close. Give him a calm, friendly picture to look at."

Aaron did as the blacksmith asked. The ox eventually calmed down and the shoe was attached. "Done," sighed the blacksmith. "Thank you for your help. You can go. Tell your father his ox is ready."

"I will," assured Aaron.

When they reached Aaron's house, people were arriving for the Friday night Sabbath.

Aaron's mother came to the door. "Aaron, you are late. The sun will be setting soon and you should be getting ready for the Sabbath service."

"Matthew, would you like to stay for the service?" asked Aaron.

Matthew hesitated. "I don't know."

"I'll join your family for silent prayer some time," offered Aaron.

"Perhaps another time. I should get my father's permission first."

"I should do the same," agreed Aaron.

"Come, Aaron," ordered his mother. "Matthew, please give my greeting to your family. Tell your father my husband would be pleased to speak to him about the building of a Quaker meetinghouse."

"I will. A good Sabbath to you," said Matthew.

"Come, Aaron," repeated his mother.

"Until tomorrow," said Aaron, entering his house.

"Until then," said Matthew.

"Matthew, would you like to stay for the service?"

The Cup of Liberty

He fled into the wilderness.

Armed men were on their way to arrest Roger Williams. Williams refused to allow the Massachusetts legislature to have any authority over his church or any other. The legislature wouldn't allow anyone to challenge its authority. It wanted Williams expelled from the Massachusetts Bay Colony and sent back to England.

Williams had no intention of going back to England. He gathered up some provisions, said good-bye to his wife and children, and fled into the winter wilderness. This was no time to be traveling. The narrow trails were buried under snow and ice. Bitter temperatures caused Williams's body to ache with pain. If he didn't find shelter, he would freeze to death.

Fortunately, a Wampanoag Indian hunter came upon Roger Williams. He was weak. Williams asked the hunter for help in the Wampanoag language. The hunter brought Williams back to his village. The supreme chief of the Wampanoag, Massasoit, offered Roger Williams shelter. Williams had traveled among the Wampanoag many times. He had learned their language, and he respected their way of life.

He wrote, "I could never discern [discover] that excess of scandalous [disgraceful] sins amongst them [Indians] which Europe aboundeth with. . . ."

Roger Williams believed that it was wrong to force Indians to accept the English religion. He believed that the Puritans should follow their own faith with passion. If the Puritans treated Indians with mercy and justice, as all people were supposed to be treated in the Puritan faith, then the Indians would accept that faith.

For now, Roger Williams gratefully accepted the Wampanoag's hospitality. He was very ill. For several weeks he rested and pondered his past. He realized he had angered the leaders of the Massachusetts Colony, but he could never have remained silent just to gain their approval.

Why were religious leaders involved in issues of trade, taxing colonists, or building roads? Religion was not a business; it was a faith.

Puritanism in Massachusetts was corrupted. He had condemned the Salem leaders for stealing land from the Indians to build their settlement instead of paying for it. Roger Williams

Colonial travelers off on a journey often packed a special food that we now call Johnnycakes. They are said to have come from Rhode Island, but since they're made with corn, the colonists probably borrowed the idea from the Indians. There's still some argument about whether the correct name is Shawnee cakes, for the tribe, or *journey* cakes, for their purpose. Either way, you can see how the name could have become Johnnycake. Like any recipe that's been around for a long time, there are also arguments about the right way to make them. Some people say they should be thick; others like them thin. Some say add sugar; others say absolutely not. Try making this version for breakfast, topped with butter and maple syrup. If you pack them for travel, leave them plain!

Rhode Island Johnnycakes
(Makes nine large cakes)

¾ cup cornmeal
¼ cup whole wheat flour
1¼ tsp. baking powder
1 Tbsp. sugar
pinch of salt
½ cup milk
1 egg
2 Tbsp. vegetable oil

1. Mix cornmeal, flour, baking powder, sugar, and salt in a medium-size bowl.
2. Add milk, egg, and oil, and mix until dry ingredients are moistened.
3. Grease a skillet or griddle, and heat it on the stove.
4. Spoon the batter into the skillet, and cook over moderate heat for about 6 minutes. Turn the cakes, and cook the other side for 5 minutes.
5. Serve warm with butter and maple syrup.

called for a separation between religion and the government. Religious leaders shouldn't control the government. He also called for an end to forcing people to become Puritans. Only those people who believed in Puritanism should join the faith. For Williams's beliefs, he was almost arrested. He was forced to leave the colony, but he wasn't discouraged.

When he felt strong enough, Williams was eager to build a house so he could send for his wife and family. A few other men from his Salem congregation joined him at the Wampanoag village. They also were eager to clear land and build a new future for themselves.

Massasoit showed Williams the surrounding land. Their journey led to the village of Canonicus, the chief of the Narragansett. It was here that Williams repaid Chief Massasoit for saving his life.

Chief Canonicus was upset with Chief Massasoit. Massasoit wanted to be independent of the Narragansett, but that wasn't possible without breaking treaties both chiefs had agreed to honor. Williams worked to secure a compromise. When a compromise was reached, Massasoit granted Williams land to build a settlement on the east side of the Seekonk River.

Roger Williams was overjoyed, but his happiness soon faded. The Plymouth Colony told Williams the land Massasoit had granted him was under the Plymouth Colony's control. If they let Williams build a settlement on this land, it would destroy the friendship between their colony and the Massachusetts Bay Colony.

Fortunately, Roger Williams was able to exchange the land rights with the Narragansett chief for another section of land on the other side of the river. This land became the new colony of Rhode Island. Here all people would be allowed to practice their own faith without fear of persecution. Here religious leaders would not run the government. That job belonged to the people.

In later years, Roger Williams stated that he believed the people of the Rhode Island Colony drank as deeply from the cup of liberty as any people that can be heard under the whole heaven.

Name This Bird

A German music teacher named Gottlieb Mittelberger moved to Pennsylvania in 1750. He wrote a small book that described the new things he saw. He was a careful observer of the varieties of trees, animals, fish, and birds that filled this new land. Can you guess what bird Mittelberger describes here?

"The most marvelous bird of all, not only in Pennsylvania but perhaps in the entire world, is a little bird rarely to be seen. This little bird is not even the size of a May bug. It is no bigger than a gold-crested wren. It glitters like gold, and sometimes it appears to be green, blue, and red. Its beak is a little long, and sharp as a needle; its feet are like very fine wire. It sips nothing but honey out of flowers, and that is why it is known as the sugar-bird. It builds its nests in some such place as the flowerpots in a garden. . . . This bird moves its wings incredibly quickly, and makes a loud hissing sound with them. . . . I won't say how much great people are sometimes willing to pay for these birds. But they do not live long [in captivity], as it is impossible to give them the food they require."

ARMS AND ARMOR OF THE 17TH CENTURY

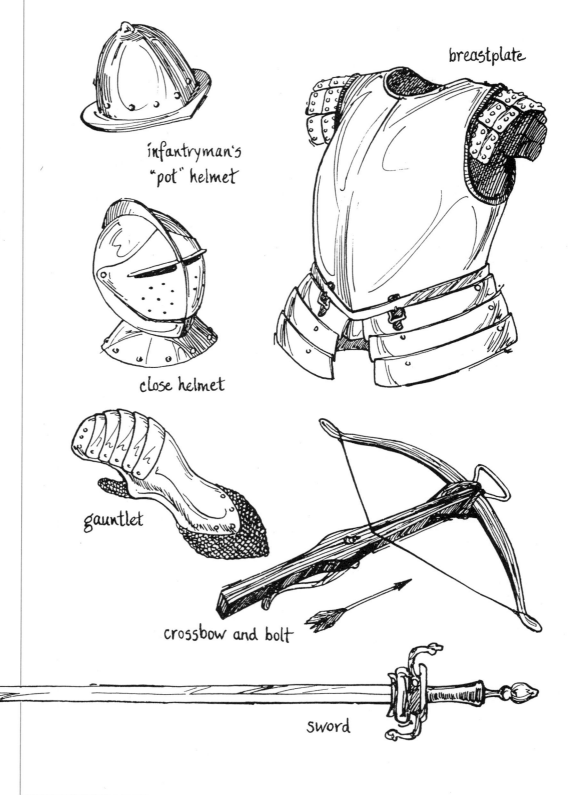

infantryman's "pot" helmet

breastplate

close helmet

gauntlet

crossbow and bolt

sword

THEY RAN THE "WALKING PURCHASE"

Among old papers, Thomas Penn found a deed to some land the Delaware Indians had sold his father in 1686. According to the deed, the boundaries had never been marked. The deed said one boundary went from the riverbank "back into the woods as far as a man can go in one day and a half." After two years of discussing the deed, in 1737 the Indians agreed to measure the land with a "walking purchase." This meant the buyers—Thomas Penn and his two brothers—would get all the land they could cover by walking at a normal rate, as the deed said, in a day and a half.

Before the day of the walk, without telling anyone, Thomas Penn and James Logan hired men to walk quickly over the land. They saw that by hurrying, the boundary could extend almost three times farther than the Indians expected. They also had the brush removed and trees chopped down, so the path would be clear.

On the day of the walk, three men quickly set out. They already knew the fastest way to go. They had horses to carry their packs and boats to take them over wide streams. Two Indians went along but could not keep up with them.

That night, one of the walkers was exhausted and dropped out. The next morning the second walker quit. Racing over the hilly ground was too much for him, too. By noon on the second day, the third walker had crossed a mountain and gone twenty miles beyond it.

According to the way a boundary had always been marked, the walkers should have gone at an easy pace and stopped now and then to relax, to have some food, and to smoke a ceremonial pipe filled with tobacco. The Delaware Indians knew they had been cheated.

Later, as Logan drew up the final map, he gave the Indians the land beyond the mountain. To him, it was barren and worthless. But he increased the new boundaries even more. Instead of drawing the line back to the river at the nearest point, he drew the map in a huge square. This added several thousand square miles to the Penns' property, and robbed the Delaware of their last good hunting lands.

The Indians were angry. Nearly fifty years of fair treatment and friendship with the white people, begun by William Penn, ended in mistreatment at the hands of Thomas Penn. The Indians could do little to get the land back. But they could unite with another nation of people the Pennsylvanians feared, the French.

Two Indians could not keep up with them.

George Washington's Warning

He spent three weeks riding through rain and snow.

What do you do when October 31 rolls around? Do you dress to frighten the ghosts in the graveyard? Or do you sit beside a warm fireplace and eat popcorn? On Halloween night in 1753, some colonists enjoyed harvest festivals, but nobody went trick-or-treating. (That custom began over a century later.)

One famous colonist was out that evening, though. Major George Washington, head of the volunteer soldiers known as the Virginia militia, was on horseback, riding to western Pennsylvania. He was going to visit the French soldiers along the Ohio River. It was no basket of treats he planned to deliver. He carried a warning letter to the French commander.

Washington always kept notes of his activities. He spent three weeks riding through "excessive Rains" and a "vast Quantity of Snow" before reaching the Monongahela River in Pennsylvania. With his assistants, an inter-

preter who could speak French, and two Indian traders, he then traveled by canoe down three rivers. Indian guides led the men through the wilderness to a French fort near what is now Waterford, Pennsylvania.

For their headquarters, the French soldiers had seized the house of an Englishman. They invited Major Washington to dinner and treated him with courtesy. But the more wine they drank, the more talkative they became. They believed they had an absolute right to control the Ohio River because a French explorer named La Salle had discovered it. They already enjoyed a profitable fur trade with the Indians, and they didn't want their rivals, the English, to get in their way. They intended to stop English families who were already beginning to settle along the river.

As British subjects, people like Washington held a different view. Not only did they believe the French were the problem, but several colonies, including Virginia, claimed rights to some of the Ohio lands.

As the evening ended, Washington delivered the letter to the commander. It was from the Virginia governor, who warned the French to leave the region. The commander wrote a reply for Washington to take back to Virginia. The return journey took almost a month. Every day except one it rained or snowed "incessantly." The horses were too weak to walk. Washington packed the letter and his other papers in a small leather backpack, and, according to a memoir written by an assistant who returned with him, Washington "put himself in an *Indian* walking dress," picked up his gun, and continued on foot. Using their only hatchet, the two men spent a day building a raft to carry them across the Allegheny River. Finally they bought fresh horses and saddles to ride the remaining distance. After "as fatiguing a journey as it is possible to conceive" they reached Williamsburg on January 11, 1854.

The French commander refused to leave the Ohio River country. A year later, armed British and colonial soldiers returned to western Pennsylvania, ready to fight for control of the land. The French were waiting for them, ready to fight back.

The two men spent a day building a raft.

Crossing the River

Sarah liked the scent in the store.

Sarah Thorpe followed her mother and father into the store on the town square in Savannah, Georgia. Like everything in the colony, the store was six months old. It was Sarah's favorite place. Once a month her family spent Saturday morning there, selecting food and the things they couldn't make themselves.

Sarah liked the pine scent in the store. She guessed today that she also smelled molasses and candle wax. The store always carried things she hadn't seen before. Smoked beef hung from hooks in the ceiling. Barrels of dried beans and heavy sacks of grain stood against the walls. Jars of pickled meats lined the shelves.

Sarah's mother reached for a painted tin of tea and set it on the counter. Mr. Thorpe was asking the storekeeper about an axe blade. In the section of fabrics and sewing notions, Sarah looked wistfully at the shiny needles. She was counting wooden spools of thread when her mother spoke.

"Hello, Polly," Mrs. Thorpe called to a woman who had come inside.

"Good day, Eliza," Mrs. Miles replied with a smile. "Mr. Miles and I have news to tell you. Can you come for tea after supper tonight?"

Sarah couldn't wait. The Miles family lived on the lot beside theirs. Sarah sometimes wished their three little boys were girls. Sailing from London on the ship *Anne*, Sarah's mother and Polly Miles had become friends.

Sarah wandered outside and stood in the sunshine. In her ragged clothes, she was almost always cold in London. But here the sky was clear, and she loved the trees and red soil. Each family in the colony was given a house of its own and fifty acres of land. Sarah's father would never go to jail again for not being able to pay his debts.

After the storekeeper recorded what they took, the two families left together. Sarah fell into step beside her father, just in time to hear a remark that puzzled her.

"But, Charles," her father was saying, "we all agreed to the laws of this new colony. Once the land is cleared, it will get easier. We'll prove that a colony can succeed without slaves and rum drinkers."

"You're wrong, Edward," Sarah's neighbor replied stubbornly. "My cousin lives across the river in South Carolina. He says the people laugh at us for doing work that slaves should do. I have sons to help, yet I will never see the profits that a slave owner can. We couldn't even clear the lands in time for planting last spring." Charles snickered. "How rich can we grow by raising tree stumps?"

"My friend," Sarah's father said, "we have such opportunity, if we just see it. But our different views must never spoil our friendship. We will come tonight and hear your news."

Sarah's stomach felt queasy. She wondered how anyone could be unhappy in Georgia. Her father worked hard and made slow progress. But he believed slaves made white men lazy.

After Sarah cleared the supper dishes, they went next door. The moon was nearly full and cast blue shadows on their path. Polly and her little boys opened the door.

"Willie," she said, "get the woolen ball for Sarah. You young ones can take turns rolling it."

Charles and Edward sat at the table. Sarah's mother and Polly crossed the room to a wooden bench beneath the small window. Sarah knelt beside her mother and arranged her skirt so it would catch the ball. The children giggled when she rolled it. They scrambled to send it back.

Mrs. Miles began hemming a shirt. Sarah soon forgot everything but the game she was playing.

"Edward," said Charles, "I meant no criticism this afternoon. But I have thought about the Georgia Colony. Across the river from us, South Carolina prospers. It's because they own slaves. But here we can own only fifty acres. A man cannot get ahead on that. And just last week, the colony was fined because we sent an empty ship back to London."

"What you say is partly true, Charles, but we cannot give up. Governor Oglethorpe chose this site well. We have begun a good fur trade with the Indians. And silk and olives will be profitable in a few years. Stay. In time you'll see I'm right."

"Like you," Charles replied, "I had nothing in London. Georgia has also been my chance to start over, and I am glad. But I am impatient. My decision is made. That's what I must tell you. Tomorrow I will see the governor and tell him, too. I am taking my family and crossing the river to South Carolina."

THE LAST OF THE FIRST THIRTEEN

The Georgia Colony, settled in 1733, was the last of the original thirteen English colonies founded in America. It was established as a place where "one hundred miserable wretches" could make a new start in life. Many of the Londoners who settled Georgia had been sent to jail in England for owing debts and were later released. In Georgia they were given land, food, houses, clothing, and farm animals. In return, they agreed to several things. There would be no slavery, no rum, and no lawyers in the new colony. The colonists would raise mulberry trees for silk, which they would export to England. Georgia would be the only colony where the colonists did not govern themselves. Why were these rules made? The *trustees*, the committee that established and governed Georgia, believed that if the colonists owned slaves, they would not learn to do hard work themselves. If the settlers were allowed to drink rum or other spirits, as alcoholic beverages were called, they would be lazy and careless. If they could hire lawyers, they would not learn to argue for themselves. It seemed wise to cultivate silk, since mulberry trees grew wild in Georgia and England imported the expensive fabric from many countries around the world.

JAMES EDWARD OGLETHORPE

James Edward Oglethorpe, the founder of the Georgia Colony, grew up in a wealthy family. He had never gone without anything. But he knew what happened to those who couldn't pay their debts. He had a close friend who couldn't pay the money he owed. His friend was put in prison.

At that time, prisons were dark, damp, and unhealthy. Germs spread easily. While Oglethorpe's friend was locked up, he caught a disease that killed him. To James Oglethorpe, the law seemed cruel.

When he became a member of Parliament, Oglethorpe worked to change prison laws. He saw that locking people up kept them from being able to work and pay their debts. He began to think he should start a colony for hardworking people who had experienced bad luck.

Oglethorpe's idea became popular. King George II granted him permission to take 150

UNITED STATES POSTAGE

1733 1933

3 GENERAL OGLETHORPE 3

This commemorative U.S. stamp, issued in 1933, honors General Oglethorpe. He was admired for his leadership and the thoughtful acts he performed as governor of the new Georgia Colony in 1733.

poor families with him to America. The king made Oglethorpe the governor of the new Georgia Colony.

It was said that during the voyage to America in 1733, Oglethorpe's thoughtfulness touched everyone. He shared food from his private kitchen with expectant mothers. He sat with sick passengers so they would have company. He helped a family plan a christening celebration for their new baby. As such stories of his kindness spread, Oglethorpe came to be admired by people everywhere.

When they arrived in Savannah, the colonists worked together to build their houses. But Oglethorpe pitched a tent and slept outdoors until all the other homes were built. When money ran short, he spent his own fortune to help buy things the colony needed.

When most of the Georgia settlers had homes and life in Savannah was going smoothly, Governor Oglethorpe turned to his next task. In 1736 he built Fort Frederica on Saint Simons Island. He assembled a small army of colonists from Georgia and South Carolina to defend colonial lands from Spain, England's rival in the territory south of the colonies. To the west of Georgia, Oglethorpe kept his eye on the French, who also wanted to crowd out the English colonists.

From 1739 to 1742, Oglethorpe led his soldiers over Indian trails through forests and swamps. They fought well against the Spanish. They protected Fort Frederica and kept the Georgia Colony safe from invasions. But they

Mary Musgrove and the Colonists

A young Indian princess, Coosaponakeesa (koo-sah-pon-ah-KEE-sah), lived with her family in what is now Georgia. Her uncle was a powerful Creek Indian leader. He knew that strong ties of trade depended on peaceful relations with the trappers and settlers who used their lands.

Coosaponakeesa's uncle thought she would make a good wife for Johnny Musgrove. Like Johnny, Coosaponakeesa was half English and half Creek Indian. After their wedding, she took the name Mary.

Mary and Johnny Musgrove began a trading post at Yamacraw, a small village that overlooked the Savannah River. When the Georgia colonists arrived in 1733, the store became a place where the Creek could trade deerskins, corn, and other things for gunpowder and beads they could only get from Europeans.

Mary Musgrove spoke English and welcomed the settlers. To help them talk with the Indians, she translated for them. Thanks to her, Chief Tomochichi and Governor Oglethorpe could talk to each other. Her friendship with the governor and her honored position among the Creek made it possible for the Indians and colonists to live peacefully for a long time.

were not powerful enough to capture St. Augustine, the oldest Spanish settlement in Florida. In spite of this, General Oglethorpe's popularity as a military leader matched the admiration he earned as governor, and made him one of the most well-liked leaders in all the colonies.

When Oglethorpe returned to England in 1735 to take care of some business for the colony, the story spread that his mother was an Indian. Indians who lived in the area that is now Mississippi wanted to see him for themselves.

Oglethorpe was gone for two years. When he returned, the Indians came to visit him. They were disappointed when they met the tall, slender, pale Englishman. Oglethorpe knew he couldn't do anything about his looks. But it is said that he told them, "I am an Indian in my heart."

In 1742 England had so many problems with her neighbors France and Spain that Parliament had no time for smaller problems in the colonies and no money to send them. Oglethorpe continued attacking the Spanish, but he spent his own funds to equip the soldiers. In 1743, when another officer accused him of making the soldiers pay for their own supplies, Oglethorpe was told to return to London and face charges. He was found innocent, but it marked the end of his career in Georgia.

He did not retire quietly, however. He worked for the welfare of soldiers and, once again, prisoners. At the age of forty-eight he married Elizabeth Wright. The same year, he led a small company of volunteer soldiers to stop an invasion of the Dutch. In 1752 he retired from Parliament, and he spent the next thirty years enjoying the company of London's great writers. He loved to discuss the changes taking place in the English colonies, which seemed to be moving into a period of rebellion. Oglethorpe died in 1785 at the age of eighty-eight.

"I am an Indian in my heart."

A Red Beard and a White Leaf

The man could send his thoughts on a "white leaf."

King Tomochichi, an old Yamacraw Indian chief, greeted the Georgia colonists with genuine friendliness. He was curious about them. Even before he agreed to sell land to them, he welcomed them warmly.

He and James Oglethorpe grew fond of each other, as though they were brothers. The first time they talked, Tomochichi led Oglethorpe through the pine trees to a high bluff overlooking the river. The Indian pointed to the Yamacraw burial ground, where he said the remains of another great Indian chief lay buried.

Tomochichi told Oglethorpe a story about a visitor his people had met 200 years earlier. A strange white man with a red beard had paddled up the stream in a small boat. When he arrived at the Yamacraw village, Tomochichi said, he had shown great friendship toward the Indians. He wanted to give the chief "a piece of curiosity" he had left on his ship. He wrote a message to the ship's officer and asked the Indians to deliver it. Soon they returned with the object the stranger had sent for.

The chief was amazed that the bearded man could send his thoughts on a "white leaf." The people thought a man with such powers might be more than an ordinary being.

Read All About It

Like all colonial newspapers, the *South Carolina Gazette* was filled with news that came from England. But it was one of the best papers in the colonies because it also printed poetry and good writing by South Carolinians. In 1734 it published a lively little verse that poked fun at some of the rules the new Georgia colonists agreed to obey. Here are some lines from that poem:

> *. . . furnish us still with*
> *whatever we've need,*
> *Provide us with bread with*
> *beef and with pork*
> *For we've never the least*
> *Inclination to*
> *work. . . .*
>
> *The King it is true has*
> *provided us Lands*
> *But what signifies that*
> *unless he'd find hands*
> *To make use of the same: as*
> *for us tho' we're poor*
> *You'll never persuade us to*
> *work we are sure. . . .*
>
> *We cannot abide this*
> *drinking all Water*
> *So beg, to your Bounty*
> *you'd add some small*
> *beer*
> *As you know you did freely*
> *enough the last year.*
>
> *Consider our case now, and*
> *pray sirs be civil*
> *Or else we shall wish you*
> *all kick'd to the D---l.*

Tomochichi continued his story. When the old chief was near death, he told his people to bury him on the spot where he had talked with the stranger. That is how the burial ground was chosen.

Oglethorpe thought he knew the name of the red-bearded man that Tomochichi described. He guessed it was Sir Walter Raleigh, the English explorer who founded the Roanoke Colony in 1586 and who sailed the eastern coast of North America. We know from old accounts that Raleigh did have a red beard, but he did not sail as far south as Georgia.

Many years later, a report was found that described French expeditions into this part of North America about 1565. The report identified the red-bearded visitor as a French captain named Jean Ribault. An explorer who knew Ribault wrote that he "was easie to be knowen by . . . the great bearde which he weare."

The Indian chief probably didn't know the name of the red-bearded stranger, or what Ribault had asked the Indians to bring back from his ship. Tomochichi didn't know what the white leaf was, either, or how someone could send thoughts on it. But you can probably guess what it was.

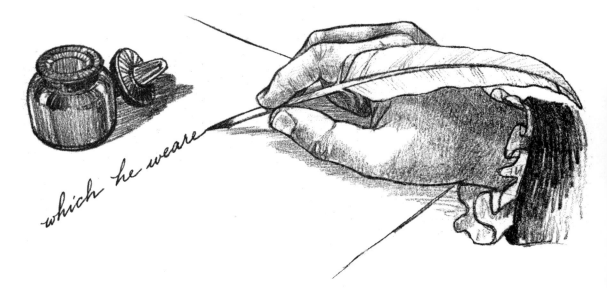

EXPERIENCE WAS A TOUGH TEACHER

The Georgia settlers found that life in the new colony was far from perfect. Yet when they complained about their problems, others laughed and called them the "Grumble-tonians." But many of their troubles were serious. The black mulberry trees that grew wild in Georgia were the wrong variety for raising silkworms. The colonists planted white mulberry trees, but they found that silkworms still grew poorly because of Savannah's changeable climate.

The trustees hoped the fifty-acre limit on property would allow each family to work its land independently, but the colonists wanted slaves to help cultivate silk. Many families moved to South Carolina, where slaves were allowed. The restriction on rum and other alcoholic beverages didn't work, either. Rum was imported illegally and laws against drinking were ignored.

The colony was supported by contributions from England, especially from the trustees themselves. They believed silk production would eventually make the colonists independent, but each year they sent more money and supplies from England.

For fifteen years, the colony struggled to survive. But finally the trustees faced the truth. Many people had already left the colony, and those who stayed often protested the restrictions. In 1752 the trustees gave up the charter, leaving Georgia the poorest and least populated of the thirteen colonies.

Natural Dyes

Colonial women spun wool and coarse cotton into yarn to make cloth for their families' clothing. They colored the yarn with dye that came from boiling wild plants in water. They knew how to make certain colors, and they experimented to get others. Indigo blue was the only dye they bought. Wherever you live, you can make natural dyes. Try dyeing some yarn and stringing a necklace with beads.

You Will Need:

Plants (list below); an ounce of white wool yarn (sold at craft stores); Woolite soap; water; scissors; newspapers; a saucepan that is not made of cast iron or aluminum (iron and aluminum will react with the dye and change the color); tongs; and beads, shells, or a crystal.

1. Go hunting for berries, blossoms, and leaves. (Gather only plants you know, and avoid private land.) Gather two or three cups of each specimen to make your dyes. Some suggestions to try are geranium petals, forsythia blossoms, goldenrod blossoms, raspberries, blackberries, and blueberries. Oak bark, tea leaves, coffee beans, and onion skins will also produce dyes. Colors will vary with the season and the strength of the plant, so enjoy experimenting with several dyes.

2. Wash the yarn in Woolite and rinse it out. Cut it into 30-inch strands. Divide them into small batches to try several colors.

3. Cover a table with newspapers to absorb spills. Put a batch of dye material (called "dyestuff") into three cups of warm water to soak for a few minutes. Using an enamel-coated or stainless-steel pot to boil the dyestuff, bring the water and the dyestuff to a gentle boil, and reduce the heat to medium. Add the yarn, and leave it in the dye for 15 to 30 minutes. For different shades of the same color, take some of the yarn out after 15 minutes, and leave the rest for half an hour.

4. Use tongs to lift the yarn out of the hot dye. Rinse the yarn in warm water, and spread it on newspapers to dry. It may pick up bits of matter from the dye—just pick them out. When the yarn is dry, string beads, shells, or a crystal on it. Finish the necklace by tying small decorative knots in several places, and one strong knot that catches the ends.

Trading Lives

They were cleaning and scraping the pelts.

Indians had engaged in trade for thousands of years before the arrival of Europeans. When the Dutch, French, and English arrived in North America, they were most interested in trading with the Indians for beaver pelts. There was a great demand for furs in Europe. Beaver hats were especially popular.

Indians hunted beaver for white traders because they were able to trade for iron products, such as metal knives, fishhooks, cookware, and weapons.

Indians didn't know how to produce metal products. However, when they got the opportunity to use such things, they saw no reason to deny themselves the chance to make their lives easier. In the process, they changed their lives forever.

"Grandfather!" exclaimed Jumping Cricket. "Why are you here? I thought you were with my father and the white traders."

"I have no interest in their conversation. The white men may speak our language, but they use it for a dishonorable purpose. When white men trade they give up little and get much in return. They seem to live only for profit. Our people trade to get what we need. My grandson, trading is a joyous event. It should bring peace and friendship. Trading with whites brings only misfortune."

"But Grandfather," protested Jumping Cricket, "what about the many knives, the axes and fishhooks, and the powerful weapons our village has now? Trading with whites has made our lives easier."

"And what of the many beaver that were killed for these axes and weapons?" asked the grandfather.

"We are at war with the beaver, they have plotted against us," Jumping Cricket insisted. "The beaver are everywhere. They have stolen the waterways, Grandfather. Ponds are drying up. Even the Great Spirit is angry with the beaver for not living well."

"And because of this we must break our vows with the beaver?"

"What vows?" asked Jumping Cricket.

"Has your father told you nothing? Man has agreed to honor the spirit of the beaver by taking no more than we need. In return, the beaver has agreed to give up its life without resistance."

"Look at all the beaver in our village, Grandfather," said Jumping Cricket. "They are not resisting us."

The grandfather looked at the women and girls sitting in the sunshine beside mounds of beaver carcasses. They were skillfully skinning the animals and cleaning and scraping the pelts. On some pelts the women added decorations. Other pelts were sewn into robes.

"Yes, look at all the beaver," suggested the grandfather. "Your mother and all the other women and girls of our village are so busy skinning animals they have no time to gather nuts. The squirrel families are gathering nuts, but not our families."

"Grandfather, there is no need to worry. We can trade for the nuts."

"There is no need to trade for nuts," the grandfather said angrily. "All we have to do is gather them. It is a dishonor not to collect the nuts the trees have grown for us."

Jumping Cricket said nothing. He was unsettled by his grandfather's mood. He had never before heard anger in his grandfather's voice.

The grandfather placed an arm around him. "We cannot continue to hunt this way. The beaver will become so angry they will leave us and never return."

The grandfather hoped his warning would make his grandson pause and see the dishonor all around him. But Jumping Cricket was staring at his father, who approached with a new musket on his shoulder.

"That is a mighty weapon," said Jumping Cricket.

"You will see how many beaver it will kill," said his father.

"Are we going hunting again?" asked Jumping Cricket.

"Tomorrow."

"Can we take Tiny Fingers? We spend so much time away hunting that I miss my brother."

"No. He is too young to fight."

"To fight?" questioned his son.

"Yes, we are going to push the Huron out of their village."

"Why?"

"Because there are many beaver to the north where the Huron live. There are no beaver left here. Come. We must prepare ourselves for the battle."

The grandfather watched his son and grandson. He was filled with sadness. His son had lost his way. He had forgotten his vow to the Great Spirit and the beaver.

The Disrespectful Beaver

In the 1600s many Indians believed there were too many beavers living on the eastern coast of North America. Wherever there was water, there were beaver dams. These dams caused streams to dry up and kept Indian villages from getting water.

The Indians believed beavers were once an ancient people and lived on dry land. But the beavers misbehaved, so the Great Spirit forced them into the water to be food and clothing for man.

This belief that beavers were disrespectful was why some Indians thought it was not wrong to destroy the beaver population.

More Beaver Died; More Indians Died

Warfare had always been a part of Indian life. But as the fur trade grew, warfare between Indian communities increased. The desire for beavers created fierce rivalries between Indian groups.

Rivalries quickly became wars. The Indians used powerful European muskets, obtained in trade, to attack their enemies. More Indians died in battle than ever before.

"That is a mighty weapon."

Making Connections

Indians were skillful hunters. But it wasn't just because Indian hunters were accurate archers. Indian men also knew well the ways of the animals they hunted.

They studied their prey. They learned where animals made their homes, what time of day they rested, and what time of day they looked for food. They observed how the animals moved through the forest and how they reacted when being chased. Indian hunters believed the animals they hunted were beings very much like themselves.

What do you know about the animals living around you? Take the time to pick one animal group that lives nearby, like squirrels, blue jays, or deer.

Follow this animal group. Take along a journal to write down your observations. Divide the pages of your journal into various categories of study, such as movement, feeding, play, family, home, and defense. Leave several free pages in the front and back of your journal for opening and concluding statements.

Each day write down your observations in the appropriate study category. Begin each daily observation by recording the date, time of day, and weather.

Before you begin this project, write down the following heading at the beginning of the first two free pages: WHAT I KNOW AND THINK ABOUT (NAME OF ANIMAL GROUP). Under this heading, write down what you know about the animal group you have chosen and include your personal opinions about this animal. For example, do you respect the squirrel? Do you consider it a friend? Do you think squirrel families behave like your family?

After two weeks of observations, review your comments at the beginning of your journal. Write down the following heading, at the top of the last two free pages: TWO-WEEK-OBSERVATION REVIEW.

Think about the following questions and write down your responses. Has your opinion about your animal group changed since your observations?

How? Do you now see similarities between the squirrels and your family? Give examples. Has a bond of friendship developed between you and the animal group?

Think about yourself as a hunter. How easy would it be to hunt and kill as many squirrels as you could, having spent time observing squirrels?

Indians believe in hunting just enough animals to guarantee a family's survival. This belief is based, in part, on the respect Indians developed for their animal neighbors. Perhaps, through your observations, you too have made some new friends.

James's Education

He plunged into the creek.

White Children Adapt to Indian Life

In colonial times, it was not uncommon for white boys and girls to live in Indian villages. These children had been captured by Indians during raids on white settlements.

White children were taken in by Indian parents who had lost children in war or to disease. Indian parents gave white children the same love that was given to any Indian child.

Many of the white children captured by Indians readily adapted to Indian life. Girls learned to farm, gather food, cook, repair houses, weave mats, and make deerskin clothing and pottery.

Boys enjoyed an adventurous education. They learned how to use a bow and arrow, how to fight, and the ways of the animals they would hunt for food and clothing.

Both boys and girls appreciated the fact that Indian parents rarely physically punished their children.

James yawned and rose from his mat. His adopted Indian father placed an arm around his shoulder and led him outside.

The sun was barely visible. The morning air was cold, and so was the water in the creek. That was where eight-year-old James and his Indian father were going. For months they had gone to the creek at dawn.

"Is it necessary that I go into the creek today?" James asked.

"Yes, and tomorrow and the days after," said his Indian father.

When they reached the creek, James stopped. He looked at the thin sheet of ice that had formed overnight.

"Why must I do this?" James questioned.

"Because you must, if you want to survive. I know no other way."

James braced himself for the shock of the ice-cold water. He let out a deep sigh and plunged into the creek. When James was fully immersed in the creek, his father sat down and puffed on his pipe.

"The water is not as cold as I feared it would be," James thought. James was learning to brave the cold.

The Indian father signaled James to dive into the water and then come out. Wet and cold, James could see the smoke coming out of his house. He desperately wanted to go inside and sit by the fire, but he knew he couldn't until he was dry.

His adopted father was toughening James's body. He was teaching James that with the proper education he didn't need layers of English clothing. He could learn to be warm in winter by being covered with bear grease and deerskin.

"You are not shivering as much as you used to," stated his Indian father. "You will not need to fear the winter, my son." James's Indian father smiled.

When he was dry, James raced home to sit by the fire and eat a meal of smoked bluefish and a bowl of corn mush and molasses. Finished with his meal, James grabbed his bow and his pouch of arrows and raced outside to his classroom—not inside a house but outside, in the woods. Another hunting lesson was beginning. James watched the other boys checking to see where the sun was in the sky.

"The deer have just finished their morning feeding," stated one boy.

Beyond the village, the boys found a patch of matted bushes and plants. Deer had slept here last night. They checked for clues that might reveal the deer's path.

James found several broken branches. Another boy found a deer track. An older boy knelt down to examine the track.

"Is it not a deer track?" James asked.

The older boy laughed. "Of course it is, but I want to know how big this deer is."

"How can you find that out?" James questioned.

"A large deer has passed this way."

"By measuring how deep the track is. See," said the older boy, placing his finger in the track, "it covers more than half my finger, and the ground has not been softened yet by the sun. A large deer has passed this way. There is the deer," the boy said quietly. "Spread out."

James moved out to the right of the deer, along with another boy. Suddenly the deer bolted by them. The two boys raced to string an arrow in their bows.

The other boy released his arrow first. It missed the moving deer by quite a distance. James released his arrow, but his hair got caught in the string. The arrow traveled several feet and fell harmlessly to the ground.

James and the other boy laughed. James had learned another lesson. He would have to shave half his hair off, like the other boys.

Later, as the day ended, the boys returned to the village. James would remember what he had learned today. Every fact, every day, helped bring him closer to the time he would kill his first deer. On that day he would join his adopted father and the other hunters. It was a time he looked forward to.

That night, as the air grew cold again, James and the other children gathered around the fire to listen to an elder's stories of Indian heroes and their bravery.

James fell asleep listening to the elder's history lesson. He dreamed of being a hero, and his story being told around a fire on a cold fall night. His early life among whites was an ever-fading memory.

A four-year-old boy from Pennsylvania was taken by the Iroquois (IR-eh-kwoi) people. He grew up to become an Iroquois chief named Old White Chief. Old White Chief said the following about his life:

"The last I remember of my mother, she was running, carrying me in her arms. Suddenly she fell to the ground on her face, and I was taken from her. Overwhelmed with fright, I knew nothing more until I opened my eyes to find myself in the lap of an Indian woman. Looking kindly down into my face, she smiled on me and gave me some dried deer meat and maple sugar. From that hour, I believe she loved me as a mother. I am sure I returned to her the affection of a son."

The colonists had to build their own schools and provide room and board for the teacher. Because money was scarce, the teacher received property from the parents in lieu of a paycheck.

This wooden hornbook, so-called because transparent horn protected the vellum text, was used by a child to learn the alphabet and the Lord's Prayer.

COLONIAL SCHOOL DAYS

Every colony tried to provide a school for its children. Sometimes it was a Dame School, called this because the teacher was an elderly widow. (In those times, a married woman was called Dame Smith rather than Mrs. Smith.) "School" was an extra room in her house, where children came for their lessons. In the southern colonies, large plantations meant towns were farther apart. Sometimes the school building was thrown together in the middle of an abandoned tobacco field. (George Washington rode horseback twenty miles each day to attend one of these country schools.)

In New England towns of fifty families or more, the parents were expected to pay for and build a school. Some fathers cut logs for the frame or to burn in its fireplace, while other families provided room and board to the teacher during the school year. Rather than a paycheck, the teacher (who was more often a man than a woman) might get a cow, chickens, hay, apple cider, or other property from parents.

A day in a colonial school wasn't anything like it is today. No music, no art, no hot lunch, no recess, no dances or after-school programs. Even worse, there were no books or desks! Students sat on long benches all day, copying the alphabet, spelling words, or arithmetic problems onto a thin layer of animal hoof, called horn, fastened over a paddle-shaped board. The board had a hole in the top and a cord, so the students could wear the "hornbook" around

their necks. (An unexpected benefit was that a teacher never heard the old excuse "I lost my book.") Lunchtime often lasted two hours—enough time for pupils to walk home and back.

Most colonial schools didn't mix boys and girls. It seems strange to us now, but the men who made the rules for schools thought girls didn't need anything more than simple reading skills. Some girls who were lucky went to public school for an hour early in the morning and again in the evening when the boys had gone home. But well-educated colonial fathers usually made sure their daughters learned everything their sons did. Tutors and private schools for girls soon became more common.

Colonial kids didn't chew gum (there wasn't any), but if they misbehaved they were sent outside to cut a whipping switch from a small tree. Or the branch might be slit at the end and the student wore it on his nose. Sometimes teachers hung signs around their students' necks that advertised their crimes, such as "Bite-Finger-Baby" or "Lying Richard."

TWO LESSONS IN ONE

While colonial boys were at school, girls had their own lessons at home. Sewing was one of the most important skills they learned. As wives and mothers, they would stitch their families' clothing by hand. Special clothes, quilts, and pillows were often embroidered with expensive silk thread. Fine handwork was the sign of an accomplished woman.

The first important sewing project a young girl completed was her *sampler*, a sample of all the stitches she could do. Worked carefully on the best fabric the family could afford, a girl's sampler combined sewing and spelling lessons all in one. It included each letter of the alphabet, both capitals and lowercase styles, her full name, the date she finished it, and sometimes a verse from the Bible or a short poem. A decorative border often finished the piece, and it was usually framed in wood and hung on the wall for everyone to enjoy.

Today, old samplers in good condition are treated as treasures. They are expensive and hard to find. Reproduction samplers are available in kits, with the lettering stamped on the cloth in ink as a guide to follow. Colonial girls had no such guides. They stitched slowly and carefully, trying to be patient as they did their best work.

Sample This

A colonial sampler is an ambitious project for beginners. Starting with just your name and the year will give you an idea of how a colonial girl spent much of her time. The most popular stitch was a cross-stitch, sewn like the letter X. Ask your mother or another grown-up to help you draw the Xs in pencil on your fabric.

You Will Need:

An eighth of a yard of white or natural muslin or linen, a ruler, a pencil, a plastic spring hoop, three skeins of DMC embroidery thread (called floss) in your three favorite colors, a size 12 embroidery needle, and sewing scissors.

1. Rinse the fabric in warm water. Press it flat and dry with a warm iron.

2. Woven fabric has a grain, or a direction to the weave. Look for the horizontal line of thread, and place your ruler on it as a guide. With a pencil and the help of a grown-up, copy the Xs that spell the letters of your first and last names (from the sample letters here) onto the cloth. Each X should be about ⅛ inch tall. The Xs in a single letter should connect (see illustration). In the center space below your name, draw Xs to make the year. Make a border of Xs above and below your name and the year.

3. Separate the rings of your hoop, and place the fabric over the smaller ring. Adjust the fabric so the Xs above your name are near the center of the hoop. Place the outer hoop over the fabric and pull the fabric gently until it fits snugly. If it is tight enough,

it will not pucker as you stitch. If it loosens as you sew, adjust it.

4. Separate three strands of embroidery floss from the rest of the floss. Thread your needle, and tie a knot in one end of the thread. As you sew, keep a long tail on the thread so it doesn't slip off the needle.

5. Cross-stitches are made with two stitches of the needle. Beginning with the top row of Xs, practice making them until you get the technique. Start with your needle behind the hoop. Poke it through the fabric at the lower left corner of the first X. Let go of the needle. Bring your hand to the top of the fabric, and gently pull the needle and thread forward. Position the needle at the top right corner of the X, and push it through to the back. Come up from the back again, at the lower right point of the X. Gently pull the thread through. Push the needle down into the fabric at the top left point of the X. You have just completed your first cross-stitch. In traditional cross-stitch, you begin at the left so the right half crosses on top.

As you work, keep your stitches snug but loose enough so the fabric doesn't pucker and wrinkle. At first it takes time to find where to start the needle and how tight to pull, but you will learn. If you make a mistake, slide the needle off your thread, and carefully pull out the stitch you just completed (you can't easily pull others out, though, so be sure you're happy with each one before you start the next).

To make the next stitch, begin in the lower left por-

tion of the X as you did before. (It's great if you can find exactly the same hole you used to begin the second half of the first stitch—that is, on the lower right side—but if you come close to it, be satisfied for now.) Bring the needle up to the right again, and go down through the fabric at the top of the pencil line. From the back of the fabric, bring the needle up at the bottom right, and push it through at the top left.

Continue each X in the same manner until you have finished the row. From time to time you will need to separate the hoop and move the fabric so you are always working near the center of the hoop. Before your thread becomes too short, turn the sampler over and run the needle through a row of stitches to hold it in place. Clip the thread, and rethread your needle with three strands of floss.

For extra practice, complete the bottom row of Xs. Separate the hoop, position the fabric correctly, and sew each stitch as before. When you are not working on your sampler, store it with the floss in a clean plastic bag.

To begin the letters of your name, change the color of the floss. When you finish one letter, begin the next, as long as you have enough thread. Always work with three strands. When you finish your name, change to the third color and stitch the year.

When your sampler is done, you might want to add more rows of stitches to the border. Just take the fabric out of the hoop and use a pencil to draw more rows of Xs. After the stitching is done, use a steam iron or damp cloth to press your sampler on the wrong side. Protect it in a wood frame and hang it on your bedroom wall.

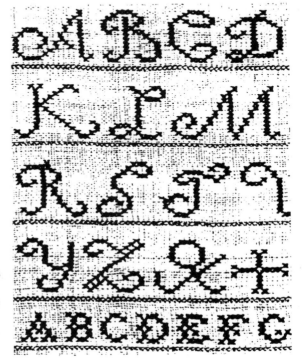

Colonial Manners

"Jeer not nor affront them."

An important duty of colonial parents, just like parents now, was teaching their children proper behavior and manners. One handy guide they turned to was a little book that came from London. *The School of Manners* was first published in 1701. Here are some of its suggestions for children:

1. "When any speak to thee [you], stand up. Say not I have heard it before. Never endeavor to help him out if he tell it not right. . . ."

2. "Run not Hastily in the Street, nor go too Slowly. . . . Throw not aught [anything] on the Street, as Dirt or Stones. If thou [you] meetest the scholars of any other School, jeer not nor affront [insult] them, but show them love and respect and quietly let them pass along."

Those are still bits of good advice. But the rules that follow show you how some of our eating habits have changed since the eighteenth century.

3. "Bite not thy [your] bread, but break it, but not with slovenly [dirty] fingers, nor with the same wherewith thou taketh up thy meat."

4. "Dip not thy Meat in the Sawce."

5. "Take not Salt with a greazy Knife."

6. "Spit not, cough not, nor blow thy Nose at Table if it may be avoided; but if these be necessity, do it aside, and without much noise."

7. Lean not thy Elbow on the Table, or on the back of thy Chair."

8. "Stuff not thy mouth so as to fill thy Cheeks; be content with smaller Mouthfuls."

9. "Blow not thy Meat, but with Patience, wait till it be cool."

How many of these have you heard from your parents? Which ones have changed, and why? What advice would you give kids if you were writing the new School of Manners book?

Get together with a friend and write your modern rules. Fold a few sheets of plain paper in half to make a booklet. Print one or two rules on each page. To give your book an old-fashioned look, draw a large, stylish initial letter for the first word of each rule. Illustrate the book with drawings of kids obeying the rules.

CHECK YOUR CALENDAR

After 1582 colonists such as the Dutch, Germans, and French, who came from the European continent, counted days on the Gregorian calendar. The independent-minded English, however, stuck with the Julian calendar (named for the Roman ruler Julius Caesar) until 1752. Under the Julian calendar, the English began the new year on March 25. The same date on the two calendars was eleven days apart! Can you imagine how confusing things were?

As long as everyone stayed on home soil it was fine. But picture life in America. Travelers in the colonies had to know which calendar was used where and be very organized or risk arriving eleven days late (or early) for an appointment!

On September 3, 1752, Great Britain and her colonies decided to switch to the Gregorian, or New Style, calendar. September 3 on the old calendar was September 14 on the new one. The English solved this problem by just skipping eleven days to catch up!

The calendar still wasn't uniform, though. In the Delaware Valley, Quakers and Congregationalists changed the names of the days of the week because they didn't like the references to pagan gods. The day we call Wednesday, for example, was Woden's day, the day that honored Odin (later spelled Woden), the ruler of the Norse gods. Our Thursday was once Thor's day, for Thor, the Scandinavian god of thunder.

The Quakers switched the names to numbers, beginning with a day devoted to God. A Quaker child said she was going to First Day school instead of Sunday school, and a Saturday trip to the market happened on Seventh Day.

"Stuff not thy mouth."

Fox and Geese

If you live in a wintry climate, you know the fun of leaving your footprints in a sparkling fresh snowfall. Fox and Geese is an old winter game to play on a day when the snow is high and you're tired of being indoors. It's also a good game to play on a sandy beach, or even in an empty parking lot, using sidewalk chalk to draw the lines.

You Will Need:

Several friends; a snow-covered field, a beach, or a safe parking lot; and sidewalk chalk (only if you must draw the game circle rather than make it with your feet).

1. Make tracks with your feet in the snow or sand (or draw it with chalk) that form a large circle. It can be any size—25 to 50 feet across, or as large as you want it.

2. Tracking with your feet again, divide the circle into eight or ten sections, like a pie.

How You Play:

1. One person agrees to start the game by being the "fox." The fox stands in the center of the circle. All other players are "geese." The geese may stand anywhere in the circle, but everyone, even the fox, must stay within the lines at all times.

2. When the fox cries, "Run, Geese!" the game begins. The fox chases the geese around the circle until he or she tags someone.

3. When the fox tags a goose, the fox yells, "Stop, Goose!" and that goose becomes the new fox.

4. The new fox goes to the center of the circle and cries, "Run, Geese!" and the game continues. The game is over when everyone decides to stop playing.

A New England Farm

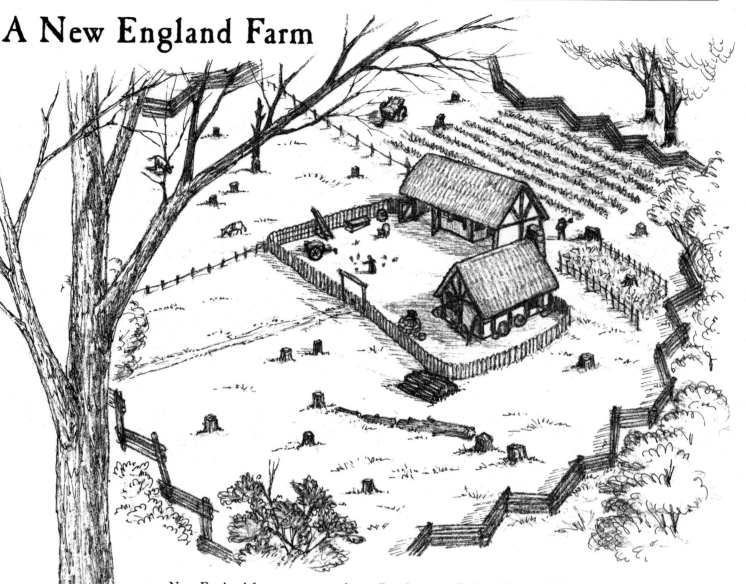

New England farms were much smaller than the plantations of the southern colonies. If you've ever helped fell a tree or chop wood, you know what's involved. A man like Samuel Winslow could clear two acres a year—leaving the tree stumps, that is. When he died, his sons might inherit a hundred acres and a woodpile—his lifetime's work.

At first, the forest was cleared by chopping trees, but soon farmers discovered a faster way to kill a large stand of trees. The method was called girdling. With a sharp tool, the farmer cut a ring through the bark that went completely around the trunk. The tree died slowly. As the leaves withered, the sun shone through from above. It provided the light needed for the crops that would replace the forest. The dead trees looked eerie, but girdling saved time and made it possible for the farmer to plant food for his family right away.

Before Farmer Winslow planted, though, he fenced his land. Just as he hurried to clear the field, he had to build fences quickly, too. An old saying described a good fence as "pig-tight, horse-high, and bull-strong." The popular split-rail, zigzag fence stood about four feet high. Also called a "snake" or "worm" fence, the split-rail fence did not require digging deep post holes. It was easy to build, repair, and move to another section of the farm if necessary. It kept out goats, sheep, pigs, horses, and cows. The first of these animals were brought to the colonies from England.

The colonists knew nothing about "high tech" farming. They used hand tools like shovels, spades, and hoes. Oxen-pulled plows—designed and made by the farmer himself—appeared in the 1700s.

Early colonists like Winslow took farming lessons from the Indians. The most important rule was simple: plant corn "when the white oak leaves reach the size of a mouse's ear" by dropping some kernels into a hole and fertilizing them with dead fish.

To many Indian tribes, corn was sacred. Farmer Winslow had never raised it before, but he quickly understood why the Indians depended on it. His family, livestock, and chickens all survived on it. It resisted diseases that killed many other crops. A field of corn provided seven times the food he could get from a field of wheat.

Corn wasn't just food for the table. Winslow could stuff a mattress with the husks, feed the stalks to his cattle in winter, and make corncob pipes and bottle stoppers from the cobs.

When the young cornstalks stood about two feet high, Farmer Winslow copied the Indians again. At the base of the stalks he planted beans and squash—usually pumpkins. The beans climbed the stalk and the pumpkins grew in vines around the base. Farmer Winslow knew that he and his family would not have survived in the new country if the Indians hadn't shown them what to plant and how to plant it.

The heart of every colonial home was the kitchen. Its tall fireplace warmed the great room, or the main room of the house, and produced the flame that cooked everything a family ate. Above the fire hung a spit for roasting a fresh side of meat. A large iron kettle with legs sat over the coals. Into the pot went roasting potatoes, beans or vegetables for a thick soup, fruit to be cooked into sauces, or batter for breads.

Favorite recipes have always been part of a family's unique character and history. One American who must have understood this guessed that "some of the Pilgrim Fathers must have come over to this country with the Cookery book under one arm and the Bible under the other." He was probably not far wrong, either.

When you set the table for dinner, do you take for granted that you will put silverware beside the plates? If you lived in early colonial times, you'd have eaten most things with your fingers, or maybe with a clam shell scoop. When John Winthrop, the governor of the Massachusetts Bay Colony, came to America, he brought along a fork. To many people, this was an odd utensil. Even more curious, it came in its own little carrying case.

A Cookery Book

Think of the foods your family likes best. Are there special recipes that only Grandma or Grandpa makes? Have some of your family favorites been passed down from one generation to another? Did some of them originate in, or come from, another country? What are your favorites?

Begin a "Cookery Book" of your favorite family foods. Gather them in a special notebook with blank pages or one you can add to. Include foods you cook for the first time. Prepare the colonial recipes in this book and include them. Some cooks like to include the date they tried each new recipe and the name of the person or place they got it from. As it grows, your cookbook will become your own record of family history.

The Death of Blackbeard

His face was half-hidden behind a beard.

Charles Town, later spelled Charleston, South Carolina, began as a small English trading village on the coast. It was often under attack by Indians, who resented the presence of white men; by Spaniards, who wanted to push the English out and take the land; and by pirates, who hid along the coast and robbed ships that dared to sail the unprotected waters.

Sea trade between Europe, Northern Africa, the Caribbean, and the colonies grew rapidly during the seventeenth century. English, Dutch, Spanish, and French ships carried goods made at home to trade across the Atlantic.

In the 1600s England passed laws that barred the colonies from trading with foreign countries. The English also slapped high duties, or fees, on rum that was shipped to the colonies from Caribbean islands, and on tobacco, indigo (a popular blue dye), and other colonial products.

Shipbuilding increased, especially in Virginia and Massachusetts. As more ships sailed the oceans, there were also more rules about sea trade and higher duties to be paid on goods. Piracy became one way dishonest men could ignore trade laws and avoid paying duties. A fleet of pirate ships could overtake a lone trade vessel, steal its cargo, and sell or trade it illegally to dishonest merchants.

One of the most feared—and fearsome-looking—pirates was Edward Teach, better known as Blackbeard. His face was half-hidden by a beard that hung from his cheeks to his belly. He armed himself with three rows of pistols strapped across his chest, and, if that weren't enough, he finished his "look" with a row of smoking matches stuck in his beard and beneath his hat.

Blackbeard stalked the Virginia and Carolina coasts, forcing frightened colonial leaders to pay him to leave them unharmed. He hid out in river inlets where he could see, but not be spotted by, approaching ships.

In 1717 Blackbeard captured several colonial ships near Charles Town. Desperate for first-aid supplies for his crew, he boldly sailed into the harbor and demanded a medicine chest. He threatened to burn the town and kill his prisoners if he didn't get it. He did.

A few months later Blackbeard's ship was spotted in the ocean off North Carolina. The governor of South Carolina quickly ordered two crews of sailors from tobacco ships to surround the pirate's ship.

A bloody battle began. Twelve colonial sailors were killed and twenty-two were wounded before Blackbeard was struck by Robert Maynard, an English naval officer. Maynard beheaded the pirate on the spot, tied his skull to the bowsprit, and sailed off to Virginia, where he became an immediate hero. Thirteen members of Blackbeard's crew were taken alive, tried, and found guilty in Williamsburg, Virginia. They were hanged to death on Pirate Road, as an example to others.

You'd Know Him Anywhere

Captain Charles Johnson collected the history of notorious pirates. In 1724 he wrote a book about them. This is his description of Blackbeard:

"This Beard was black, which he suffered [preferred] to grow of an extravagant Length; as to Breadth, it came up to his Eyes; he was accustomed to twist it with Ribbons, in small tails . . . and turn them about his Ears: In Time of Action, he wore a Sling over his Shoulders, with three brace of Pistols, hanging in Holsters . . . ; he wore a Fur-Cap, and stuck a lighted Match on each side, under it, which appearing on each side [of] his Face, his Eyes naturally looking Fierce and Wild, made him altogether such a Figure, that Imagination cannot form an Idea of a Fury, from Hell, to look more frightful."

They were hanged on Pirates Road.

MARY READ AND ANNE BONNY

Captain Charles Johnson called his book *A General History of the Pyrates*. It was a huge success and was printed in English, French, Dutch, and German. Two of the most unusual characters Johnson included in his pirate history were women.

Mary Read was born in England. When she was sixteen she dressed in men's clothing, left home, and became a sailor on a warship. Next she learned to handle a gun, which was useful when she became a soldier. On her way to the West Indies, in the 1720s, she was captured by pirates. Mary wasted no time falling in love with one of them. Her clothing fooled no one, but her bold behavior and swearing impressed her shipmates.

At sea in the Caribbean, Mary met up with Anne Bonny, another young pirate who sometimes dressed in "Men's Cloaths." The two women sailed on the same ship, along with the pirate Calico Jack Rackham. Anne fell in love with Calico Jack, but they were not destined to live a long and happy life together.

Calico Jack was captured in a battle with a British ship. When the attack began, the cowardly male pirates scurried below, leaving Mary and Anne to defend the ship. Anne was sorry to see her lover hang, but we don't know that she shed many tears. "If he had fought like a Man," she said, "he need not have been hang'd like a Dog."

What happened to Mary Read and Anne Bonny? Another old pirate history says that they were caught along with Calico Jack. When the judge asked why they should not be killed along with the other pirates, they both pleaded for their lives, claiming that not only were they women, they were both expecting babies. Because Mary and Anne were both telling the truth, their lives were spared.

Mary met up with Anne Bonny.

Dog's Head in the Porridge Pot

Jack's friends threw them out.

The door of The Sign of the Dog's Head in the Porridge Pot tavern opened. The smell of tobacco smoke and rum rushed out. Thirty thirsty laborers rushed in looking for a drink.

Preston Jack moved past the incoming customers toward the center of the room. A man in rags stopped him.

"Preston, good sir, buy me a drink," pleaded the man.

"It's a waste of my good money and reason. And besides, I'm busy. Move your tables back," ordered Preston Jack, holding a fighting cock under each large arm. "You heard me," he shouted at a table of uncooperative men.

The four men didn't move. Preston Jack kicked the table. The men stood up and drew their knives.

A dozen of Jack's friends surrounded the four and threw them out, two through the open door and two through the window.

"They mustn't be from our fair New York," said Preston, peering through the broken window. "Our men wouldn't go so peacefully."

The Trouble with Rum

Drunkenness was a big problem in New York and all other English colonies. By the 1760s, in New York alone there were seventeen distilleries making 540,000 gallons of rum each year. Four-fifths of all rum produced was consumed in the colonies.

Excessive drinking caused men to fight and commit unlawful acts. To prevent drinking problems, children were taught to abstain from alcohol.

Rum was also used as a weapon by white settlers. Though there was a severe penalty for getting an Indian drunk, settlers did it anyway because it was profitable.

Indians weren't used to drinking alcohol. Settlers took advantage of this situation. They shared their rum with Indians. When the Indians became intoxicated, the settlers confused them with conversation. Settlers then persuaded Indians to give up or sell their land, even though they had no wish to do so.

The people laughed. Preston Jack held up the cocks. "Gentlemen, ladies, two of the finest fighting cocks are about to battle. Only one will survive. If you be interested in placing a bet on who will be the winner, gather round."

Jacques Lemond and his Indian wife had no interest in cock fighting. They searched the crowded room, looking for a place to sit. Lemond approached a table.

"May we sit down?"

"You can, but not your Indian wife," sneered one man.

Lemond and his wife walked on. In the back, beyond a table of men playing cards, they noticed a man sitting by himself.

"May we sit down?" Lemond asked.

The Englishman shrugged his shoulders. The Frenchman took that as a yes. He and his wife sat down.

"Got an accent, don't you?" the Englishman asked.

"Yes, I do," said Lemond.

"Sounds French."

"Yes, it does," replied Lemond, trying not to say too much.

"Don't play games with me, Frenchman," warned the Englishman. "You're lucky I let you sit here. We don't take kindly to Frenchies or to New France."

"Then perhaps I should leave," commented Lemond.

"I'm sorry if my opinion offends you." The Englishman smiled, revealing three missing teeth. "Tell me, it must be hard for a few Frenchmen to watch over all that land you claim as New France. I'm surprised you're here, sir. You must be leaving thousands of acres of French land unguarded."

"Your jest is most amusing," stated Lemond.

"I'm pleased you find me amusing." The Englishman swigged a bit of rum. "But I tell you I am not amused that French fur traders have made a king's profit in New

"Only one will survive."

"This knife can be your pen."

France, with the help of Indians." The Englishman tipped his hat at Lemond's wife. "And why not? Beaver are plentiful in New France, and their fur is very handsome."

"It is indeed."

"Then you have traded for furs?"

"I have done some trading."

"Some trading." The Englishman laughed. "Where? Draw me a map, if you'd be so kind," the man requested. "As a fellow fur trader, I'd like to know."

"Sir, this must be another jest. I have no tools to write with."

The Englishman took out his knife. "This knife can be your pen, and the table can be your paper, sir."

Lemond took the knife. He thought about using it against the Englishman, then he remembered how troublemakers were treated in this tavern. The Frenchman decided this invitation to draw a map was a perfect opportunity to embarrass the English trader.

"I will be happy to draw you a map." Lemond revealed a broad smile.

The Frenchman drew an outline of North America and divided it into three uneven sections.

"This petite section is your English Territory," stated Lemond. "And here, in this grand middle section, is New France," Lemond stated proudly as he quickly carved the letters N F, for New France, into the table.

The English trader fumed with anger. He grabbed the knife from Lemond's hand and plunged it into the New France Territory.

"I think you'd better leave, Frenchman."

Jacques Lemond and his wife left the table.

The English trader glared at them and shouted, "I will visit you in New France very soon with my knife and my musket!"

The French and Indian War

The French hid among the trees.

The French claimed some of the most beautiful, most fertile land in North America. A Frenchman could proudly state that the Mississippi River was his to navigate, the fertile Ohio River Valley was his to farm, and an enormous beaver population was his to hunt.

In order to maintain this claim on this vast territory, the French had to protect their land from enemies seeking to take it. The French had far fewer settlers in North America than the English did. In 1750 there were approximately 55,000 Frenchmen and 1,200,000 Englishmen in America.

The English colonists had had enough of the French and their land claims. They especially despised the French claim to the Ohio Territory, the land west of the Appalachian Mountains. The English believed this territory was theirs.

In 1754 Britain went to war against France to take France's land in North America. This conflict was called the French and Indian War. The name "French and Indian War" was given by the English because they were fighting the French and the Indians. However, the English weren't fighting all Indian people. The Iroquois Confederacy, made up of the Mohawk, Oneida, Onon-

daga, Seneca, Cayuga, and Tuscarora people, fought alongside the English.

The opening battle of the war took place in the Great Meadows of western Pennsylvania. At stake was the possession of the Ohio River Valley. The French had built a fort to defend the valley, but that didn't deter young George Washington. He marched about 400 Virginia troops to attack the fort, which held twice as many French troops. The Virginia troops were defeated.

The next year, British General Braddock marched 2,000 troops from Virginia through steep wilderness to attack the French fort again. This time the British had enough troops. The French had only 800 men. However, General Braddock didn't know how to use his men effectively.

The French hid among the trees and fired at the British troops. The general refused to let his men leave the field and take cover. He was trained to fight by standing your ground. Almost 1,000 British men were killed or wounded in this second defeat of the war.

The first British victory happened on September 8, 1755—but it could have been another setback. William Johnson led an army of 3,000 colonists and 500 Mohawk Indians to Lake George near French territory in Canada. When a scout reported to Johnson that French troops were nearby, he sent 1,000 men to the area. The men were ambushed.

Johnson's remaining men formed a ring and readied their muskets. They waited for the French to appear. When French troops arrived, they were met by a ring of musket fire and artillery. The French forces were defeated. The first British victory was recorded.

In the coming years, British, Indian, and colonial forces recorded more victories. In 1758 they captured the French fort of Louisburg in Nova Scotia, and in 1759 they captured two French forts guarding Lake Champlain in New York. This lake provided the simplest path into the center of New France. It stretched between Canada and New York. Anyone who controlled this lake had access to French territories to the north or to the south.

The French defeats continued until the Treaty of Paris was signed and agreed to by the British and French governments in 1763. The French and Indian War was over, but not for many Indians. They were disappointed by the British victory. The French had treated the Indians fairly, and, most important, the French kept their land free from settlers. The Indian people feared the British victory would bring unwanted colonists onto their land.

The Colonies Join Together

The Atlantic Coast had changed forever. What had been a land inhabited by Indian groups living in villages was now reorganized into the towns and farms of thirteen colonies. The Iroquois Confederacy, a loose union of six Indian nations, was among many Indian groups witnessing these changes.

The Iroquois Great Council observed colonists bickering over the boundary lines that separated one colony from the other. It witnessed colonies competing for control of the land west of the Appalachian Mountains known as the Ohio Territory.

This concerned the council. It didn't want to live beside bickering neighbors. On July 4, 1744, Chief Canassatego, the elected speaker of the Great Council, told an assembly of Iroquois and colonial officials, "Our wise forefathers established union and friendship between our [Indian] nations. This has given us great authority with our neighbors. By observing the same methods our forefathers have used, you will gain much power; therefore whatever befalls you, do not fall out with one another."

The Great Council wanted the colonies to form a union. This idea was quickly dismissed. The individual colonies weren't interested in the prosperity of all thirteen colonies. Each colony cared only about its own prosperity. Each colony took pride in the right granted to it by the British king to govern itself.

The colonies were settled by people who came from such nations as Britain, the Netherlands, and Germany. They came with no money, or they came with vast sums of money. Some people came with families; others came alone. Some people came unwillingly, like the African slaves; some people came as indentured servants. The colonies were a gathering place of many different people holding many different points of view.

When the French and Indian War began, the lack of cooperation between the colonies was clear to the Iroquois Great Council. Many colonists believed it was their duty to fight the enemies of Britain because they were British subjects. But the colonists' passion to fight was weakened by the colonies spending more time arguing instead of planning.

Again, the Iroquois Great Council offered its advice. "Look at the French," said one Iroquois chief. "They are men, they are fortifying everywhere, but you English, we are ashamed to say it, you are all like women: bare and open, without fortifications."

When the French and Indian War ended in a British victory, something new emerged. It was a feeling of pride shared by all the colonies. In spite of all their bickering, the colonies did join together to defeat the French and Indian forces. The colonists found out they could work together for a common cause. Could they do it again if their independent spirit was challenged?

THE THIRTEEN COLONIES WITH THEIR FOUNDING DATES

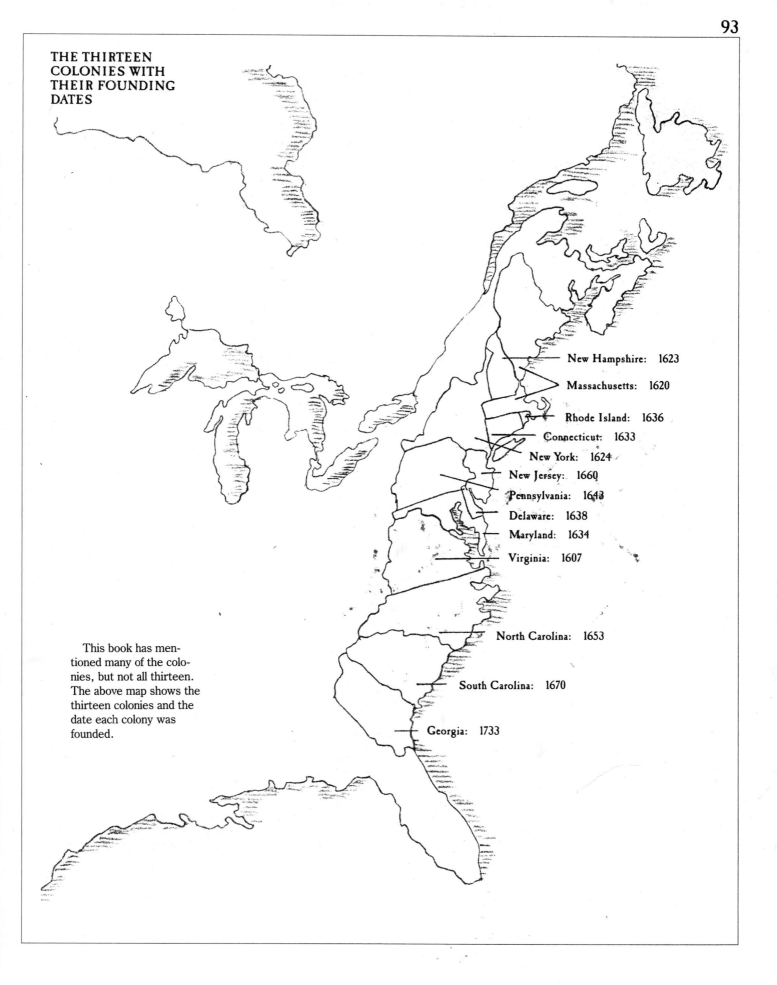

New Hampshire: 1623

Massachusetts: 1620

Rhode Island: 1636

Connecticut: 1633

New York: 1624

New Jersey: 1660

Pennsylvania: 1643

Delaware: 1638

Maryland: 1634

Virginia: 1607

North Carolina: 1653

South Carolina: 1670

Georgia: 1733

This book has mentioned many of the colonies, but not all thirteen. The above map shows the thirteen colonies and the date each colony was founded.

If You Want to Know More

The discoveries you've made in this book about the American colonies can lead you to other enjoyable and challenging information. This section lists books to read, activities to try, and trips that will help you explore other aspects of life in colonial America.

Books

You can find other good books about colonial people and their adventures. If you're not sure where to look, ask your librarian to show you how to use the card catalog or computer to find the books suggested here.

Christopher Columbus didn't have any money! He didn't have a watch! He didn't have a refrigerator! How did he do it? Read *Christopher Columbus: How He Did It*, by Charlotte and David Yue (Boston: Houghton Mifflin Co., 1992). This book provides interesting facts and answers to questions you've always had about Columbus.

It was Sir Walter Raleigh who convinced Queen Elizabeth I to establish English colonies in the New World. But why didn't he ever visit Roanoke? The answer to this question, and more about other Roanoke settlements that failed, can be found in *Roanoke: The Story of the Lost Colony*, by Peter I. Bosco (Brookfield, Connecticut: Millbrook Press, 1992). If you're intrigued with the disappearance of Virginia Dare, William H. Hooks may be just the author for you. He gathered the mysterious legends of Virginia and the Indians into *The Legend of the White Doe* (New York: Macmillan, 1988).

The Wampanoag Indians took food to the hungry colonists of New Plymouth. If the Indians hadn't shared their vegetable crops of corn, beans, and squash, the colonists would have starved to death. Although the Wampanoag Indians did not write their history, they left many clues that tell us about their homes, their diet, their clothing, and other aspects of their lives. You will find *The Wampanoag*, by Laurie Weinstein-Farson (New York: Chelsea House, 1988), a good account of this generous people, their history, and how they live today.

Would you be willing to stand up for what you believe? Would you risk your life? Anne Hutchinson, Mary Dyer, Lady Deborah Moody, and Penelope Stout did. *Four Women in a Violent Time*, by Deborah Crawford (New York: Crown, 1970), tells their stories. These four courageous women of the seventeenth century expressed their opinions in a time when men ruled, and women were expected to be seen and not heard.

Can you imagine an earthquake rattling the colonists? One of the strongest in American history shook the Atlantic states in 1755. It led to unusual theories and the first scientific writings about the earth's powerful movements. To find out how geologists are still investigating that old quake, ask your librarian to help you find a copy of *American Heritage*, volume 31, no. 5, August/September 1980. Read "The Great Earthquake," by Jourdan Houston, on pages 102–107.

The constant fighting in North America between 1689 and 1759 was called the Colonial Wars. The English, French, and Spanish fought these wars—with the Indians caught in the middle. What caused so many conflicts and how America changed are explained in *The Colonial Wars*, by Alden R. Carter (New York: Franklin Watts, 1992).

Finally, if a particular colony captured your interest and you want to explore its history more deeply, hunt up The Colony Series, published by Franklin Watts. Choose your favorite colonies and read all about them in these informative little books.

Arts and Activities

When the first colonists sat down for supper, the entire family often ate from the same wooden bowl, called a trencher. Later they had time to make wooden and pewter dishes and eating utensils. If you'd like to try working with wood, you can carve a simple wooden spoon like those found on colonial tables. For how to make your spoon, get *Green Woodworking: Handcrafting Wood from Log to Finished Product*, by Drew Langster (Emmaus, Pennsylvania: Rodale, 1987). If you haven't worked much with wood, have a grown-up help you get started. Experienced woodworkers will enjoy *Historic Models of Early America and How to Make Them*, by C. J. Maginley (New York: Harcourt Brace & Co., 1947). In this book of hand-tool projects are instructions for a Viking ship, a butter churn, a flatboat, and many other models from colonial life.

Maybe you've finished your cross-stitch sampler and you want more sewing ideas. *American Cross-Stitch*, by Hildy Paige Burns and Kathleen Thorne-Thomsen (New York: Van Nostrand Reinhold, 1974), is filled with patterns. Some of the projects you can stitch from this book are a hornbook sampler, a New England town, and George Washington. You'll also find neat colonial art projects and goodies to make for the holiday season in *American*

Christmas (Des Moines, Iowa: Better Homes & Gardens Books: 1984).

Weather vanes seem to be as popular now as they were when people really needed them to know which way the wind—and smoke—was blowing. The Vikings used them at sea to determine how to set their sails. Colonial weather vanes were usually arrows or farm animals. With the help of a grown-up assistant and the book *Folk-Art Weather Vanes*, by John A. Nelson (Harrisburg, Pennsylvania: Stackpole, 1990), you'll have complete directions for working with wood or metal and making the pole, or standard, for the top of your roof.

Have you played all the games in this book and wish there were more? Then *Games of the World*, edited by Frederic V. Grunfeld (New York: Ballantine, 1975), is right for you. If you played Fox and Geese in the snow, try it on a table with marbles. Just like colonial children did, you may have to make your board and round up the marbles. (If you do, you're in luck. Every game includes directions for making what you need to play.) There are even pages of "games to start a game." This book is packed with fun and filled with photos and illustrations from around the world. It may surprise you to learn where some of your favorite games originated.

Trips

Maybe your family is planning a summer vacation that will take you through one of the original thirteen colonies. For extra enjoyment on the trip, surprise them by taking along the Smithsonian Guide to Historic America. This is a series of beautifully illustrated travel guidebooks that combine history and travel for every section of the country. If you're going to one or more of the "colonies," stop by your library first and ask for the guidebooks for the states you will visit. You will want *Northern New England; Southern New England; Virginia and the Capital Region; The Mid-Atlantic States; The Carolinas and the Appalachian States*; and *The Deep South*.

Index